IT'S THE GOVERNMENT, STUPID

How Governments Blame Citizens for Their Own Policies

Keith Dowding

BRISTOL
UNIVERSITY
PRESS

First published in Great Britain in 2020 by

Bristol University Press
University of Bristol
1-9 Old Park Hill
Bristol
BS2 8BB
UK
t: +44 (0)117 954 5940
pp-info@bristol.ac.uk
www.bristoluniversitypress.co.uk

British Library Cataloguing in Publication Data
A catalogue record for this book is available from the British Library.

ISBN 978-1-5292-0638-8 hardcover
ISBN 978-1-5292-0639-5 paperback
ISBN 978-1-5292-0641-8 ePub
ISBN 978-1-5292-0640-1 ePDF

Cover design: blu inc, Bristol
Printed and bound in Great Britain by CMP, Poole
Policy Press uses environmentally responsible print partners.

In memory of Brian Barry

Contents

List of Tables

Acknowledgements

Stephen Wenham asked me if I would write a popular book for the new Bristol University Press. This is the one I wanted to write. It might appear to be a book on public policy, but I consider it a work of political philosophy. Political philosophers ought to be more aware of policy, and what their claims about political issues entail. This is an attempt to do just that with regard to personal responsibility.

I would like to thank Ed Handby and Alex Vuong for helping me chase down information and papers on the public policy areas for me. Various people have read chapters or the whole manuscript. I would like to thank Frank Bongiorno, Will Bosworth, Ed Handby, Andrew Hindmoor, Patrick Leslie, Matt Matravers, Lars Moen, Alex Oprea, Don Ross, Marian Sawer, Simon Stevens, Marija Taflaga, William Sanders and Stephen Wenham.

The final version of the book was written during November 2019 when I was a visiting fellow at the Center for Advanced Studies Ludwig-Maximilians Universität Munich, during part of the time I was supposed to be doing something else. I'd like to thank my host Klaus Goetz, and Julia Schreiner and Isabella Schopp, the staff who looked after me so well, for providing such an ideal place to work undisturbed.

Anne Gelling read the entire manuscript twice and offered encouragement as well as superb copy-editing of my sometimes incoherent sentences. I have a habit of missing out the word 'not' when typing frenziedly, which is about as bad an error as one can make. I think she has spotted them all. I also thank Caroline Astley and Leonie Drake at Bristol University Press for help in preparing the manuscript and dealing with editorial issues.

A note on sources. As this book is written for the general public as much as for academics I have not cluttered the text with references or footnotes. The bases for the empirical claims I make are contained in the sources listed at the end of the book collected by chapter and page number.

Politicians have recently got into the habit of apologizing for the policies of their predecessors. One day we might get them to recognize responsibility for their own policy failures and perhaps apologize for them even as they enact them.

Preface

This book was researched and drafted in 2019, and the use of data and evidence reflects that. It grew from my increasing frustration with how governments in many parts of the world, notably Australia, the US and the UK, the three countries I know best, continually blame citizens for what I see as government failure. Just as I was delivering the manuscript to the publishers in December 2019, coronavirus disease 2019 (COVID-19) was first identified in Wuhan in China's Hubei province. From the start there was some discussion in the media about how dangerous it might be and whether it posed a threat of pandemic, but this was all rather low key. As early as January 2020, some countries were taking actions against the risk of such a pandemic, but these were in South East Asia. Europe, Australia, Africa and the Americas did not seem too concerned. Some governments were planning behind the scenes, others were not.

By March 2020 it was becoming clear to everyone that COVID-19 was a pandemic that required drastic action. As I write now, in late April 2020, it is clear that governmental responses to COVID-19 have varied widely. Some countries, when they acted, did so decisively, others not. Furthermore, the strategic response has differed.

Some countries closed borders and ordered lockdowns quickly to stop the spread of the disease. Some have taken a more relaxed attitude, providing citizens with advice on hygiene and physical distancing, but have not enforced lockdowns. Singapore, for example, took early tough action on entry into the country and shut down businesses and schools. New Zealand also took relatively swift and dramatic action. Both countries, as of April 2020, have been widely praised for their actions. Sweden has taken a different line. It encouraged citizens to be careful and to maintain some physical distance, but has not enforced lockdowns. Its rate of infection and its mortality rate are both higher than in countries with stricter conditions, notably similar neighbouring countries such as Norway and Finland. As I write, Swedish experts and the government there are still defending their policies, arguing that their superior health service has not been overwhelmed as it has in some countries and that we will not really be able to tell for several years, after later waves, and economies had a chance to recover, which policy, ultimately was best.

They might be right. Issues are complex. The policies which reduce infections and death rates in the early phases might not have such good effects in the long term. All sorts of factors then come into play, such as second waves of infection; the probability of individual reinfection; the relative standard of health care in a country; and the difficulties of lockdown – it is easier for Singapore to lock down than the US, for example. Culture matters too. Furthermore, the speed of response to economic breakdown will also have effects on health, wealth and mortality rates in the long run.

This book is about the responsibilities of government and COVID-19 is a dramatic example of what a difference government can make to public welfare. Considering the different strategies from New Zealand to Sweden, for instance, provides an example of how governments might enforce regulations or simply advise and 'nudge' people towards the kind of behaviour the government considers welfare-enhancing. It shows how much power governments can wield as they ensure that people self-isolate to a large enough extent, and use some coercive measures to regulate the opening of business, insist non-essential business shut down, and prohibit large social gathering. They can do so sensitively or crudely, with a lighter or a heavier touch. COVID-19 also dramatizes the problems of government. It might seem to present a simple enough health issue. Ensure non-transmission to stop the pandemic. But doing so in the most effective manner might destroy the economy, and that will affect citizens' welfare not only through wealth effects, but through health and indeed mortality rates. Governments do not have it easy.

The COVID-19 pandemic also shows how governments with a populist and authoritarian nature can endanger their citizens, both refusing to act and disseminating false information in ways that are dangerous to the welfare of their people, and, conversely, regulating in ways that instantiate their authoritarian grip on society. COVID-19 is thus a dramatic example of how governments can fail to act, can act and regulate well, and can over-regulate. We can also see, most strikingly – ludicrously, indeed – in President Trump's wild behaviour and talk, how political leaders can try to blame others for their own failures in foresight, planning and basic leadership skills.

This book does not consider such dramatic examples of government failure. Rather it looks at longer-term, bread-and-butter issues: gun regulations, obesity, housing, gambling and recreational drugs. But the issues involved here have similar characteristics. How far are people to blame for social outcomes, and how much is government failure responsible? If you tell people not to socially gather during pandemic, and they do, how much blame does each 'social gatherer' bear? What about those who did not go to large gatherings when forbidden, but nevertheless caught the virus, so must have interacted with someone who did? Do they bear any blame for that? To be sure, if people do gather, you can say society has failed, and you might point the finger at those who went to major events, or who did not change their lifestyle, and laud those who self-isolated. But while those who self-isolated are less likely to catch coronavirus, the fact that others do not still increases their chances of infection. One cannot blame an individual just because they caught COVID-19.

The argument of the book is that while there is individual responsibility with regard to our behaviour, the major responsibility for social failures is that of the government. The relative success in terms of health following the COVID-19 pandemic will be that of the government, not individuals. Those countries with better health services (relative to other countries similarly economically placed) are likely to fare better. Those that act decisively (no matter what decisions were taken) are likely to fare better. And yes, some decisions will be better than others, though here, blame is harder to assign; one must consider the evidence available at the time, as well as the final outcome.

The bread-and-butter issues that I write about in this book – such as obesity and homelessness – can be described as social failure. These failures are not the simple ones that we might see with COVID-19, for they are not failures of one major political actor, but rather of government over many years, with different political elites in control, different parties in power, different ideologies. However, over the past 50 years one specific over-arching ideological viewpoint has dominated. And that is the cult of personal responsibility, propagated not only by politicians but also by moral and political philosophers. This cult has enabled governments to blame their citizens for their own policies. I argue in this book that government has increasingly placed responsibility on citizens for that which is the government's own responsibility.

1

Responsibility

Recent decades have seen a rise in homelessness through much of the Western world. In Australia, levels increased by almost five per cent from 2011 to 2016. On census night in 2016, 116,000 people were homeless; that is a rate of 5 per 1,000 people. Who is responsible? 'Get a good job that pays good money', said Joe Hockey, the Australian treasurer, to young people complaining they could not get a start in the inflated housing market – or get your parents to buy them for you, the Australian prime minister chipped in.

Gun crime in the US frequently makes headlines around the world. Between 2014 and 2018, according to the Gun Violence Archive, there were 71,429 deaths and 113,947 injuries in gun-rage incidents: an average of 14,286 deaths and 22,590 injuries per year. Who is to blame? Again, according to some leading US politicians, it's citizens who are to blame. The bad guys. Guns don't kill people, people do, the argument runs (and some of those killers are only three years old). Some go further and say the solution to gun crime lies in more weapons: 'The only thing that stops a bad guy with a gun is a good guy with a gun'.

Obesity levels are rising sharply internationally. In the UK about 28 per cent of the population are thought to be obese, with a further 35 per cent overweight. In the UK obesity is estimated to reduce life expectancy by about three years. Obesity costs the National Health Service (NHS) about £5 billion per year, with the costs to the economy estimated to be £27 billion per annum. The government response to growing obesity is health campaigns advising people to be careful about what they eat, and to take more exercise. It is as if the rise in obesity has nothing to do with modern methods of food manufacture developed in the 1960s and 1970s; methods that the government has barely regulated. It is the choice of people to eat the food that is widely available in the shops, not the government that regulates what is sold in shops, that is to blame for the obesity crisis.

Governments like to blame us for the woes of society. They like to blame their citizens. But if people can rightfully be blamed for the choices they make from the menu of alternatives available to them, they cannot be blamed for the menu itself. If we want to know who to blame for the range of options that exist for us, then we have to look at society; and the biggest and most important agent in that social choice of the menu of opportunities is the government. Who is responsible for the housing and homelessness crisis, the number of gun deaths and the growing amount of obesity in society? It's the government, stupid. That is the argument of this book.

Looking back

Following the great depression of the 1930s and then in the aftermath of the Second World War, governments acted to look after the health and welfare of their people. They regulated markets, built houses, provided public utilities and enacted regulations to protect safety and consumer rights. In short, they took on responsibility for the health and welfare of their citizens. One reason for the popularity of the welfare state, particularly in Europe, is that war had affected all classes of people, and it was obvious that people's dislocation and welfare losses were due largely to how lucky or unlucky they had been in the war. The welfare state helps to pool risk, and the war was something everyone was in together. Certainly, providing public housing when so many people had lost their homes from extensive bombing seemed an obvious task for governments.

To be sure, not everything was perfect. There will always be some problems with government policies and provisions, along with claims of inefficiency. Government is subject to the kind of media scrutiny over what it does on a daily basis that no firm in the private sector ever receives. Unforeseen and unintended consequences and planning disasters mean that governments are often blamed for the results of their policies – though not all 'planning disasters', as the Sydney Opera House attests, are seen as such by posterity.

Post-war governments saw their job as being to provide for the welfare of their citizens and they were judged on those terms. By the 1970s it was generally felt that the welfare state was here to stay. However, the oil price shock and other events led to increasing claims that government had got too big, too inefficient and needed to be slimmed down. The process of getting the government out of the provision of services, indeed out of seeing its role as looking after the welfare of its citizens, had started.

In this process, it was recognized that, once the initial infrastructure had been created, various public goods – clean water provision, telecoms, gas and electricity utilities – could now be run for profit. Technical innovation also made it easier for the market to operate, with rival companies providing electricity or gas within the same neighbourhoods using the same infrastructure. Now various public goods and utilities, for which there had been market under-provision (so-called 'market failure'), could be marketed successfully and profitably. Government welcomed pressure to privatize, seeing that private investment could replace public, thus easing tax problems, and that it had the added advantage that any failures in provision of such goods were now at one remove from government itself. Government could shift blame to the private providers, needing only to be seen to re-regulate rather than having to actually solve the problems. A process of privatized blame-shifting was utilized by government to get out of the business of looking after the welfare of their citizens. Armed with the political philosophers' universally proclaimed need for people to take responsibility for their lives, government could also shift blame for social problems to individual citizens. The cult of personal responsibility was born.

Now that government did not have to take the blame, individuals could be held responsible for all their own ills. This enabled so-called deregulation. In fact, the deregulation of the 1980s onwards is a myth. What happened was privatization and re-regulation. The regulations changed, but there weren't fewer of them. On the contrary, as you privatize public provision and then provide oversight, especially in areas where the provision is non-competitive, the complexity of laws and regulations governing the industries involved tends to increase. At the very least, one set of regulations is replaced by another set. But what deregulation usually implies is that government regulates not with the welfare of consumers in mind, but rather with the welfare of service providers. So, over the past 40 years, the growing trend in society has been for governments to pull out of taking direct responsibility for the health and welfare of their citizens. They have thrust responsibility back on to individuals.

Bizarre as it seems, government no longer appears to see its role as looking after the welfare of its people. Of course, few who work in government would agree. The bald statement is too much for them to bear. However, we have increasingly seen politicians claiming that citizens must take responsibility for their own lives and their own decisions, often in the popular guise of reducing taxes to allow people to make their own decisions and keep greater control of their own lives. Politicians have taken the lead from those critics of the welfare state who argue that government intervention was creating people who did not take responsibility for their own welfare. They were making unrealistic demands and had unrealizable expectations. The state was too paternalistic, treating citizens as children rather than allowing them to take responsibility for their own lives. The nanny state was causing problems rather than solving them. Such critics argued that we need to get the state out of running so much and let the private sector and the market take over. Then individuals could make their own choices, take responsibility for their own welfare and everyone would be better off.

The idea that citizens shouldn't take responsibility for their own decisions and choices seems as crazy as the idea that government shouldn't bother to try to promote the welfare of citizens. But can both government and citizens be responsible for the same thing – personal welfare? The answer is yes. Thinking that either one or the other has to take responsibility is to mistake the *level* at which each must be responsible. People can only be rightfully held responsible for the choices they make from the menu of opportunities available to them. I cannot be held responsible for not selecting a course of action that I have no reasonable opportunity to choose. What governments can do is to extend and vary the menu of opportunity for their citizens. Through their regulatory and spending decisions, governments supply both the number and the distribution of opportunities.

Moreover, people are subject to various forces: evolutionary, economic, social. We are increasingly becoming aware of these forces: mechanisms that operate at both the individual and the social level. At the individual level, we have a growing understanding of how our biology and neurology work, of how evolution has shaped us to desire certain things and make certain sorts of decisions. The problem for modern people is that our society and technology have changed so much that some of the characteristics that formerly served us well are now damaging us. Evolutionary shifts in our biology cannot keep pace with technological change. Worse still, businesses and industries, for their own ends, use these facts to manipulate people. It is government's job to understand these forces, and to act to try to ensure that their citizens are not exploited. Each of us can only rightfully be expected to take responsibility for what is 'up to us'. As Robert Kane suggests, this means when we could have chosen otherwise and when 'the ultimate sources of actions lie in us and not outside us in factors beyond our control'. If others manipulate our choices, then we lose some of that 'up-to-us-ness'.

So there are two sides to personal responsibility. The first is that we can only be responsible for the choices we make from the reasonable set of alternative possibilities that are open to us. The second is that we can only be held responsible to the extent that we are not subject to forces that are reasonably beyond our control.

As we shall see, governments do tend to recognize the second aspect, but only in restricted domains. They acknowledge that addiction is a physical illness that demands medical intervention. They accept that people suffering from addiction or other pathological behaviours are not fully responsible for their actions and the appropriate state response is to provide some assistance. They are belatedly beginning to recognize the range of aspects of life in which people are subject to addictive behaviours. Even then, however, governments tend only to acknowledge issues which affect small numbers of people who behave in ways that most others do not. As we shall see in Chapter 5, for example, gambling addiction is now recognized as a medical condition and governments are beginning to accept they have a role in helping addicted citizens. What they are reluctant to acknowledge are those forces that affect everyone; the particular appeal of excess salt and sugars in food, for example. It is not that we cannot decide to avoid certain sorts of food and drink, but the great attraction of the excess quantities that firms have discovered exert mass appeal are not 'up to us'.

Governments are much less keen to admit that the population at large can suffer welfare problems when natural human behavioural forces are subject to incentives that our nature is not used to. When it comes to issues such as diet, it is not just the 5 per cent or so of the population that are vulnerable to addictive forces who are susceptible, but everyone, leading to growing health and obesity problems around the world. Furthermore, these natural behaviours are used by firms to sell their products. And we cannot blame them for doing so. The competitive market is such that if one company uses our knowledge of what will make children buy fizzy drink and another does not, then the latter will lose its market and go bust or be taken over. Economic and social forces lead to firms manipulating people. Where this occurs, we should not blame either consumers or producers. It is the government that regulates the economic and social world and the government that must bear responsibility.

Governments have not faced up to the fact that, while individuals can reasonably be held responsible for the choices they make given their opportunities, they cannot be reasonably held responsible for the opportunity set itself. Government can reasonably be held responsible for the opportunities that citizens have, for government is responsible for setting the rules and regulations that determine those sets of opportunities for people. And those opportunities do not have to be set once, early on in life. They can be established to ensure that people have opportunities to better themselves at various stages in their life, no matter how bad their previous choices were. I will discuss these aspects of responsibility in this chapter.

In this book I will be looking at a set of selected case studies and will argue that, overall, the welfare of people in liberal democracies has greatly diminished as governments have got out of the business of looking after their citizens. Over the past 40 years or so, governments have not only failed to keep up with what is happening in markets that serve their citizens badly and failed to regulate in ways which are socially optimal, but they have actively pursued policies that have created more social problems. They have acted in ways that make people less, not more responsible for the lives they lead. We will see this particularly in Chapter 4 on housing policy. Here governments have done two things. First, they have largely abandoned the business of providing social housing. Second, they have implemented tax incentives that lead those with money to buy extra housing not only for themselves ('holiday homes' and the like), but also to rent to others; worse still, there are even incentives that make it financially worthwhile to own properties and leave them empty. Not only has the housing crisis thus created reduced the menu of opportunities for accommodation for people, it has the knock-on effect of diminishing their opportunities in other aspects of their lives.

We can only see how these opportunities are changed through making comparisons. Comparisons show us that it is the nature of the regulations that government puts in place that creates the differences in outcomes we can see across different policy domains. The first of the case study chapters, on gun crime, offers the starkest example of how the amount of crime is dependent upon the regulations that government makes.

Before we turn to the case studies, however, I want to examine the ideology or philosophy behind the move towards government getting out of the business of providing for the welfare of its citizens. Behind that move is the liberal – or rather libertarian – idea that people should be free from state interference and take responsibility for their own lives. Government's role should be to enhance their opportunities and choices. This leads to the idea that the responsibility for social problems lies with people and not the government. So, in this chapter, I want to explode the myth of personal responsibility for society's ills.

Society's ills, its failures – or successes – are the responsibility of government. They are the responsibility of government because that is what government does. It governs. It can choose what regulations to put in place and what not to. It sets the incentives for agents – whether they be collective agents such as firms, or individual people – to act in one manner or another. In doing so, it sets the context in which citizens make decisions. That is not to say that people should not take responsibility for their actions. However, we need to put into context what people should be taken to be responsible for and what they should not. I will lay out the grounds for that case in this chapter.

Personal responsibility

A great deal of philosophical literature examines the relationship between what is in our control and what is determined. We need not concern ourselves with those thoughts other than to acknowledge, as we have, that addictions are problematic for free choice, and that there are other forces, as we have seen, that affect our decision making more, perhaps, than we would ideally like. Beyond these considerations, generally speaking, how much personal responsibility we assign to people is based upon our expectations of the reasonable courses of action they have, and that is relative to their circumstances. So, if two people whose starting positions are much the same end up with very different lives, then we may suggest that these two people can be held responsible for the differences in their outcomes.

Imagine two boys, Dennis and James, who are neighbours and whose family backgrounds are similar. That is, they come from stable households with their parents holding down decent jobs with good incomes. At first, in primary school, both boys do well, but in high school their lives diverge. Dennis starts messing around, using his wit to annoy the teachers and getting into trouble with the school authorities. He hangs out playing games with friends, does not do his homework assignments, and starts drinking and taking soft drugs. There is some trouble with the police, but he avoids any serious penalties. Nevertheless, he leaves school with no qualifications to speak of and ends up in casual employment with few prospects. As he gets older, his drug and alcohol habit increases. He finds it increasingly difficult to hold down a job, eventually can't afford the rent for his apartment, and at 35 he ends up sleeping on the streets.

James is very different. He works hard at school, avoids the sort of trouble young people sometimes get into and leaves school with good grades. He manages to get into a good university, works hard there, meets a similarly hard-working partner and gets a good job. The pair save, buy a nice house in the suburbs, choose to have a couple of children and James ends up with a good family life and earning capacity.

Now we can make the standard comparison, the sort that people make all the time. We can congratulate James and blame Dennis for where they end up. Indeed, James and Dennis might do that themselves. James can look back with quiet satisfaction at his choices. One day, seeing his old friend and neighbour living rough, James is shocked. But talking about Dennis with his partner, he says that Dennis was always a bit wild, always making bad choices and in some ways ended up with what he deserved. Dennis in fact agrees with this assessment. When asked by an academic who is researching the lives of the homeless, Dennis takes responsibility for his actions. True, he suggests that school was unsympathetic to him, and blames an early failed relationship with a girl for drinking too much early in his life, but he admits that he took drugs because they made him feel good, and that he should have worked harder at school and should have tried harder to get a decent job. "I've made a lot of bad choices," he tells the researcher, "I've only myself to blame for ending up on the street."

When we make these sorts of assessment we are assigning personal responsibility comparatively. We have two people whose circumstances were once very similar but, as their lives proceeded, they diverged. We can assign responsibility for that divergence to the sets of choices that each made during his life. Dennis could have changed course early on at high school, when his teacher first brought up his bad behaviour at parents' evening. He could have started again when he left school, perhaps, had he taken stock and used his parents' goodwill to get himself some training for a trade where he could make a good living. And he did not have to drink all that alcohol or take those drugs. Similarly, James faced many temptations and passed up some opportunities, some of which might have led to a different, better life. He is glad he avoided some of those possibilities, a little bit regretful about others, but he was more concerned with stability and achieving a contented life than with the rewards that taking risks might bring.

We find these sorts of stories used by the press, by the public generally and by the government to blame people for finding themselves living rough on the street. We look at the growing number of homeless people and say, look, had you made choices more like James's, then you would not be living on the street. And homeless people often agree. They agree because they make the same sorts of comparisons I have made between Dennis and James. However, Dennis is not to blame for the number of homeless people. Dennis is only to blame for being one of them. Responsibility for the number of homeless lies with those whose policies and regulations lead to that number. We can blame society or, as I will do, the government. The government is to blame, or to be praised, for the level and statistical distribution of rewards and benefits in society.

We should also note that in this story, while Dennis made many bad decisions, not just one, over time the alternatives available to him start closing down. By the time he had been living rough on the streets for a while, he was unlikely to have the opportunity to get a job. Gaining employment requires being able to maintain personal hygiene – one needs access to washing facilities and clean clothes for the interview. In order to apply in the first place, one needs access to a computer and, often, a fixed address in order to be able to complete the form. In some major cities, rents are so high that even those who hold down jobs are increasingly finding it difficult to keep their homes. Furthermore, it is getting more difficult for those with low educational attainments to get jobs as the number of such jobs decreases and they become less secure. Even if Dennis is responsible for ending up living on the streets, once there he might not be held responsible for not being able to leave them. He has no alternative. As we shall see in Chapter 4, drinking alcohol and taking drugs and living rough are correlated, and we can reasonably assume that drug taking is a major cause of homelessness. But once on the street, taking some comfort in alcohol or drugs might seem a reasonable alternative to sleeping rough and not drinking.

Two lessons should emerge from all this. We should not judge how responsible people are without considering the opportunities they had available to them. Furthermore, we should not take a snapshot of opportunities at any particular point in time. How Dennis ends up at 40 is not dependent simply upon a choice he made at 16, but on later choices too, and those are dependent upon the opportunities he had at later times. In my story, Dennis made many poor choices, but we do not know his full set of possible options at each stage. We should also remember that our judgement of Dennis's responsibility is only valid in comparison with someone in a similar situation, at the start of the story: James. We might compare Dennis at 23 with, say, Jane, who was then in a similar situation, but who managed to get free of drugs, go back to education and live a better life. This is the right comparator for the bad decisions made by Dennis at 23, not with what James was doing at that time. And here we need to think about what our reasonable expectations are. Our reasonable expectations about James at 23 should be based upon what people like him at 23 tend to do. The question is 'how many drug addicts at 23 kick the habit?', and not 'how many people at 23 do not take drugs when they are 24', nor is it 'how many drug addicts manage to kick the habit?'. We find, for example, that older people, those in their thirties, are more likely to overcome addiction than people in their twenties.

The second lesson is that it is wrong to take Dennis as a paradigm for rough sleepers. In my story, Dennis came from a good home with caring parents. That is not typical of rough sleepers. If we want to think about the responsibility that rough sleepers have for their condition, we need to have the right comparator, and that can only be done statistically. We need to look at the background of rough sleepers. We need to consider the social class, education levels, family background, gender, region and various other characteristics of rough sleepers against those of the general population. Differences in the statistical distribution of rough sleepers from the rest of the population in all these factors has nothing to do with the responsibility of those rough sleepers for ending up in the condition. These differences are attributable to the structure of society. No individual is responsible for the degree of the problem nor its distribution. We can lay responsibility for them at the door of our society. Since society is a collective body, and since we hire governments to solve the difficulties of collective action for such moral and social problems, responsibility lies squarely with government itself.

It's the government's responsibility

In many ways, when it comes to thinking about responsibility, it does not matter what conclusion we come to with regard to free will and determinism. The only thing that matters is that people respond to incentives. We know that consumers respond to price signals, and they respond to the quality of products. We know they respond to advertisements and other forms of information. Moreover, psychologists have shown that people respond to the manner in which items are described. This process is called 'framing'. How choices are framed can help determine the choices we make. Advertisers are well aware of that, as are charities and governments. People respond to government regulation. In fact, in society all of the responses people make are, to some extent, a response to government regulation. In that sense, everything that happens in society is the responsibility of the government.

Even in 'natural disasters', we can blame government for the degree of adversity caused, both in terms of the government response and in terms of the regulations that were set in advance of the disaster striking. How destructive an earthquake is, for example, depends upon the construction regulations that were set and enforced for the buildings, roads and infrastructure that were built in the years preceding the quake. How badly a drought affects a country depends upon the foresight of the government in setting up water distribution systems to deal with such an eventuality, how swiftly and decisively it acts when the drought bites, and so on. How bad floods are and where they occur results at least partly from where flood defences have been built and what has been built on flood plains. In recent years in the UK, towns that had not flooded for hundreds of years have done so partially because flood waters could no longer spread relatively harmlessly further upstream. How much we blame the government for the consequences of natural disasters depends, of course, on our expectations. Our expectations for the ability of buildings to withstand earthquakes are much greater now than in the past, for example, because construction engineers know so much more about how to make buildings quakeproof.

This might seem unfair to government. Can we really, after all, blame government for everything? One way of assessing government failure is to compare what life would be like without government. A large part of economics uses this thought. The first of the fundamental theorems of welfare economics suggests that competitive markets lead to the efficient allocation of resources. The idea is that firms provide products and those that are desired by the public get bought and the less desirable ones do not. Some firms therefore sell more than others. Firms look at each others' products and try to produce more of the goods that people want more. Such firms compete directly with each other, driving down prices. So consumers get what they want at the cheapest prices, which enable firms to make a profit. That is good for everyone. As Allen Feldman put it, 'laissez faire leads to the common good'.

Hence it is concluded that government ought only to interfere where there is market failure. Market failure occurs for all sorts of reasons, which generally lead to a situation where there are not enough firms to provide variety of choice and to compete with each other to drive down the price of the product. However, it is often argued that we should not assume that government ought to intervene even when there is market failure, since governments fail as well, and government interference where there is market failure might have worse results than the original market failure.

The problem with this argument is twofold. First, the fundamental theorem assumes many facts about social life that are never true. It assumes that there are no transaction costs. Transaction costs are all those costs associated with buying and selling. I've mentioned one already: the size of the market. However, important transaction costs include information. It is all very well saying that consumers will buy the product they want the most, but they have to find out what that is. For simple, cheap goods, one can find out by sampling several different varieties. We can buy apples from different grocery stores, try different types of toothpaste, and so on. However, one buys a house, if not for life, for a very long time. One needs careful examinations and a lot of information to make a reasonable decision. One cannot try out several different pension schemes before making a firm decision. So informational costs vary. There are also enforcement costs. Again, buying apples is simple, but with a complex product like a computer or a house, one needs assurance that what one has been told about its characteristics is true. When buying a service one wants some means of ensuring that one gets the service promised.

The fundamental theorem assumes everyone has perfect information. It assumes that there are no monopolies or companies that can dominate markets. It assumes firms can enter and exit markets without cost. Given that these assumptions are never true, rather than seeing markets as the default, we might see them as the fault. We might say, since these conditions that would bring efficiency never hold in real markets, we need to intervene to make markets closer to the ideal than they actually are. Competitive markets tend to become dominated by a few firms. So government needs to intervene to stop that natural move towards domination. (And indeed, governments once controlled monopolistic practices much more than they do now.) If there are reasons for allowing some companies to dominate a market, then government needs to exert close oversight over them. Otherwise we get a long way away from the efficiency envisaged by the first fundamental theorem.

The issue of transaction costs, despite all the literature, is not always understood sufficiently. Transaction costs are those faced when trading in a market. They include the costs of collecting and understanding information, the costs of bargaining, of the enforcement of bargains made and, crucially, the nature of decision making. Not understanding the results of the decisions we constantly make is a transaction cost. Here government can play a major role by providing information and forcing participants in the market to supply honest and transparent information. Government can try to ensure that firms do not make use of information they have to frame choices in ways that manipulate the natural – that is, the biological – tendencies of people in ways we know are detrimental to their health and well-being.

Another way of thinking about this issue is to realize that all markets, all of society, operate within a system of rules and regulations that is set up and implemented by government. When markets fail, they do so because government has regulated them improperly. It might have imposed regulations that are too strict or too lax. It might have interfered too much or too little. All market failure is government failure. And if that seems unfair on our political leaders, we can also point out that all market success is government success. Keech and Munger, who provide the idea that we can consider all failures as government failure, try to imagine what optimal government might look like. They realize, of course, that just as the first fundamental theorem of welfare economics is a fantasy, so is optimal government. And it is a fantasy for the same set of reasons: that is, because of informational and transaction costs, and due to domination. Not only do we not live in a perfect world, we cannot.

Some assert that government is the major problem: we would be better off with weak – 'small' – government. Their arguments tend to rely on the comparison between our actual governments and the ideals they posit in the theoretical models. Better evidence, more scientific evidence, is gleaned by comparing actual strong governments with actual weak governments. The evidence that we do not want weak government comes from comparing societies with strong governments with those failed states which do not have functioning governments. And there are plenty of examples to choose from on this planet. Would you sooner live in Norway or Yemen? Furthermore, we must not be fooled by comparing strong democratic governments with dictatorships, assuming the latter are strong states. Usually they are not strong states; they are held together precariously by threats. More to the point, dictatorships rarely regulate markets; they corrupt them.

The sorts of comparisons we ought to make are between actual institutions in different countries. If we want to increase equality, we should look at countries that have more equal outcomes and compare their institutions; to explain unequal growth rates, compare the institutions that exist in countries with different growth rates. Of course, for complex questions such as growth, many factors come into play. In the case study chapters, I show how problems have emerged in different countries over time as they changed their institutional arrangements. Of course, other factors contribute, but we can see clear differences across countries and we can see how changing the regulations created mechanisms that cause problems. We can also see, given our knowledge of human biology, why people act as they do, and how regulations can ease some problems.

The first fundamental theorem of welfare economics and Keech and Munger's idea of optimal government might try to give us an abstract idea of what an ideal society or perfect social world might look like. However, they cannot actually give us something which we can use to make judgements about the actual world. They are entirely abstract and theoretical. Even the formula provided by the fundamental theorem cannot be used as a comparator, since we have no idea what kinds of values to plug into it. So any assessments that we need to make about how well our government is doing have to be based upon comparisons with other societies. We can judge the rules which led to the outcomes we find in our society by comparing those outcomes to ones achieved under different rules. That is the method I adopt in my case studies.

Normative political theory

As a political scientist as well as a political philosopher, I am well aware of many of the reasons for government failure and regulatory failure. There is a great deal of evidence that many of the regulations created within industries operate for the benefit of the industries themselves, rather than consumers. Strict regulation of products can help prevent new firms from entering the market, enabling those already there to benefit from less competition. Indeed, the entirety of government policies, the regulations implemented, expenditure decisions and laws, are subject to enormous pressures from organized lobby groups and other powerful interests. However, this is not a book of empirical political science, nor of the policy process. It is a book within the field of normative political theory. I shall work through some policy areas where I think we know enough of the science – both natural and social – to see the effects of government policy. I argue, then, that government needs to take responsibility for those outcomes, no matter what caused government to behave as it did.

Many of my colleagues who work in the field of political philosophy might look askance at the claim that this is a book of political philosophy. After all, political philosophy is usually conducted at an abstract level to try to give us certain principles about the manner in which we should govern society. Or it is concerned with conceptualizing basic political terms, such as freedom, responsibility, legitimacy, political power or authority. Or it considers grand questions such as the justification of there being a state in the first place and why we should follow its laws. This is all very well, but it is distanced from the real problems that society faces.

Political philosophy all too often spends far too long discussing the wrong topics. The thrust of this book is that governments blame citizens for their own policies. They have been aided and abetted in this scandal by some political philosophers who have spent too much time on individual responsibility and not enough on governmental responsibility. Too much time on analytic accounts of markets and freedom, without considering the empirics of markets and freedom. Too much time on idealizations, without realizing the first lesson of empirical social science. All inferences about the effects of institutions on behaviour, and how we can reasonably expect people to behave in different circumstances, can only be examined *comparatively*. There is a debate in political philosophy about ideal versus non-ideal theory. Too much of that is about whether we can think of ideal institutions prior to considering the empirics of institutions. So we can do our ideal theorizing and then look at society. However, we can only work out our ideal institutions when we have seen how people respond to incentives.

Political philosophy in the academy seems far too removed from politics. It is not that we should not be examining the nature of freedom, the justification of authority or what we consider to be the principles of justice. It is that political philosophers should not only be doing that. This book is a book of political philosophy, one that intends to suggest that philosophers need to reconsider their subject, move away from the constant focus on individuals and turn their attention to governments. After all, how can the proper role of governments in looking after the welfare of their citizens not be a, if not the, central topic of political philosophy?

In general, too, political philosophers need to be more aware, or at least demonstrate how aware they are, of failures in actual societies. They need to examine topics like those in this book, and turn their attention to how their thoughts and calculations about the right principles of society actually apply in these cases, alongside the likely side effects and possible unintended consequences of policies that might accrue. The lesson that political philosophers need to be aware of, as do governments, is that policy making is about implementation. Public policy is what is implemented, not what we would like to achieve with our laws and regulations. In the same way, political philosophy needs to be about what governments and societies can do, not only what we would like to achieve.

Evidence

Underlying the argument of this book is the belief that we as a society, and our governments, are – or at least should be – aware of a lot of the causes of problems in society, yet do not act to do anything about them. The chapters devoted to public policy will argue the case that we know what causes the problems in those issue areas. However, some people are sceptical. For example, we shall see in Chapter 3 (on obesity) that the scientific evidence on the relationship between sugars, fats and carbohydrates and their effects on body shape is mixed, and different studies do not all agree either on how important they are, or the degree to which they are. One response to mixed evidence is to throw doubt upon the very fact that we have any scientific evidence at all. People may say 'experts don't know anything' or 'they're always changing their minds' or 'you can prove anything by statistics'.

And such people can point to studies that do not merely qualify but contradict previous findings on, say, how sugars affect weight gain. This is the nature of scientific evidence: different studies identify different causal factors, find strong, weak or no correlations, and trace different effects. There is also debate in science, even when correlation or causal effects are generally agreed, over the precise causal mechanisms.

However, using such disagreement to do nothing is a derogation of responsibility. After all, if we are not sure how much difference sugar, fats and salts make to weight gain, and use that as a reason not to regulate or tax the amount added to foods, then we can hardly tell individuals it is their responsibility to reduce their sugar, fat or salt intake in order to lose weight. We don't know how much difference they make, the person can reply, so it would be irresponsible of me to take care of my diet until the facts and precise mechanisms are fully known with certainty.

We do know a lot, though, and the best scientific evidence overall is derived from systematic review and meta-analysis. And it is such evidence upon which I largely rely. What is systematic review and meta-analysis? Systematic review is a process that uses a rigorous and clearly documented approach to searching for research on a subject and using independent criteria to select which studies to analyze in more detail. It then appraises and synthesizes the findings of the studies reviewed. By clearly documenting the process, systematic reviews can be updated without having to start afresh each time.

A meta-analysis is a statistical analysis that combines the results of multiple studies. Conceptually similar studies might all have some measurement error or bias, but by carefully combining them, the pooled estimate can give greater confidence in the overall results. Of course, one cannot conduct meta-analysis of sets of statistical studies if they are too different conceptually – using different definitions, coding data differently – but meta-analysis can be used both on its own or combined with systematic review to give greater confidence in the results. Much of the evidence I give in this book is based on systematic review and meta-analysis (though in the references I also refer to single studies for specific claims). Systematic review and meta-analysis should answer most of the doubts of those who think that experts disagree and for that reason we should take no notice of them.

Another important way of making inferences is through comparative studies. We can compare the effects of different regulations in different countries and see what effects these have. We must do this carefully. Countries differ in many regards; hence a difference in, say, drug addiction might not be due simply to different ways in which laws are framed and implemented, but to other factors such as geographical location (nearness to production), wealth, culture and so on. However, we can adopt large-scale comparisons with country fixed effects that can help us have more confidence in our inferences. Or we can compare countries that are very alike in many ways but differ only in, say, drug laws. We can also look at specific case studies and see the effects of changing regulations over time in that country. To be sure, the effects of similar regulatory changes in other countries might not be precisely the same. A regulatory change in the UK might not have precisely the same effects in Australia; it might not be so effective for some reason – or it might be even more effective. We should expect, though, unless there is some specific reason for thinking otherwise, that these effects will be in the same direction.

Sometimes these regulatory changes look like a 'natural experiment'. Laboratory experiments standardly involve comparing across two set-ups which differ in only one regard. Any change in the outcome is then calculated to be caused by that variation. Natural experiments occur when there is no change in society that one can imagine will have an effect, except for this one change. Differences in outcomes are then inferred to be due to that change. Natural experiments are rare because society is always changing, but we can plausibly discount many facts, and sometimes we are justified in seeing a different outcome due to this regulatory change. I use evidence of all these sorts in this book (though I do not provide detailed statistical analysis; I rely upon the evidence of others that I report).

That which is to come

In the following chapters I consider certain policy areas and concentrate upon three countries: the US, the UK and Australia. The US is a major country that has led the world in development and also, unfortunately, in many of the world's ills. I have chosen the UK and Australia for less scientific reasons – I know more about those countries, having been brought up and worked in the UK for many years, and now living and working as I do in Australia. These three countries provide good examples for my argument; and I think, too, that the lessons can be applied more broadly. Sometimes I look at other countries for specific lessons, for example Finland for some innovative evidence on housing issues, and Portugal for drugs policy.

The policy areas are chosen for more specific reasons, but one could also take them as illustrations of other policy areas where governments blame citizens for their own policies. The first is gun crime. Here is an issue where the evidence on the effect of laws and regulations can easily be seen in simple descriptive statistics. The US is an outlier which shows the effects of gun laws. We can also see the effects of laws in specific US states and in other countries as the regulations have been tightened or relaxed. I use this example to show that regulation really does matter, and importantly.

I turn next to the issue of obesity. This is more controversial: while it is largely seen as a medical issue, some people push back and suggest that growing obesity rates around the world result from lifestyle choices. The issue for me is that lifestyle choice is shaped by food-manufacturing processes which are designed to make people fat. Of course, food manufacturers did not intentionally design their processes to create an obesity crisis, but the processed food market and our own biology have combined to mean that they might as well have done. And government has been complicit in this process. It is an important example for this book. Many obese people are angry that they are blamed for their body shape. They are angry that government and medical authorities constantly push out information on diet, on healthy living, on what we ought to eat, while at the same time allowing food manufacturers to push out cheap food that is designed to appeal to our natural biological instincts to gobble it up. Should eating, that very basic function, be something we have to work at to keep healthy? Or should government set conditions so we can buy food that will do us good rather than harm? As we shall also see, some people have no reasonable alternative to such manufactured food.

The next topic is housing. Like body-weight problems, the housing crisis in the three countries I concentrate upon has intensified in the past 50 years. The issues here are even more complex, involving both specific housing policies and also fiscal policy. Nevertheless, we can track the increasing problems to changes in government legislation, both in terms of making it easier for some to buy dwellings not only to live in, but to rent out or leave empty, and also of government pulling out of the business of providing affordable housing. We can see that the problems we have now in relation to those of 50 years ago are almost entirely due to government policies over that time period. The housing crisis has been caused by government actions.

I then turn to two different issues. The first is gambling, where the problems affect a smaller percentage of the population. This is an area where we might feel more comfortable blaming individuals for their situation. The direct person-to-person comparisons I discuss in this chapter are easier to make. I look at how far we can make these judgements, and how far we can blame government for the greater incidence of gambling problems, which have grown as government has eased regulation of the gambling industry. The chapter is also important for my argument on responsibility. Governments used to be explicitly paternalistic with regard to gambling policy, regulating it heavily, but they have, in the main, now relaxed those regulations. This chapter discusses how far that was a reasonable move, but also how much responsibility government ought to bear for the problems that some people get into through their gambling habits.

Finally, I look at drug policy. Why are some drugs illegal and some not? Why do we regulate drugs differently from other things? Unlike the other areas I have discussed, government is far more paternalistic with regard to drugs than it was a hundred years ago. We might ask why. Chapter 6 suggests that again government has got its regulatory processes backwards. This, furthermore, is an area where government is especially hypocritical, since many politicians, senior public servants, policy makers and law enforcement officers know that prohibiting drugs creates more problems than it solves, but they do nothing about it.

In the last chapter I discuss the relative responsibilities of people, governments and society at large, and I consider a few objections that might be raised against my arguments in this book.

Final word

There are two aspects to personal responsibility. People should only be held responsible for the choices they make from the menu of opportunities open to them. They cannot be held responsible for not selecting a course of action that they have no reasonable opportunity to choose. Second, people can only be held responsible to the extent that they are not subject to forces that are reasonably beyond their control. If someone is ill, or suffering some impairment, one might not hold them responsible for their choice. Or we do not blame someone if they do some action we think wrong if they were subject to the manipulation or control of some other agent. We might also think that someone is not responsible for a bad choice if it seemed reasonable given the information they had.

Governments tend to acknowledge the second aspect. It does so by recognizing in law that individuals might behave criminally when they are subject to threats, or need protection if they suffer from certain mental illnesses, including addiction; and they recognize that information is important when it comes to misleading claims about products. However, they tend not to acknowledge the first.

Yet people are not responsible for their choices when all the choices are bad. Society is responsible, and since government is the most important actor in society, it must bear responsibility for the menu of opportunity its citizens face. Economic and social forces tend to lead to firms manipulating people. It is the role of government to regulate the economic and social world to ensure genuine individual autonomy, and government should accept responsibility for poor outcomes. What governments can and should do is to extend and vary the menu of opportunity for their citizens. That does not constitute a nanny state. Quite the contrary: it is one that increases the freedom and therefore the responsibility it extends to its citizens.

2

Gun Crime

Nikolas Cruz was dropped off by an Uber driver just outside the Marjory Stoneman Douglas High School in Parkland, Florida, on 14 February 2018. Carrying a rifle bag and backpack, he walked purposefully into Building 12 of the school, which contained 30 classrooms and about 900 pupils and 30 teachers. After activating a fire alarm, he used his AR-15-style semi-automatic rifle and fired indiscriminately. In six minutes he killed 17 people and wounded the same number before leaving the school grounds. It was the deadliest high school shooting in US history – but it is only one of many gun massacres where ten or more people were killed, as we see in Table 2.1.

For virtually anyone who lives outside the US, it is not just the fact of the massacre and others like it that they find incredible, but also the response to such atrocities by the authorities and large numbers of citizens. It is not only the vapidly proffered thoughts and prayers – the usual response of many politicians, a knee-jerk reaction condemned by Emma González, a surviving Parkland student – but where they place the blame. The local newspaper blamed the school for not responding quickly enough to the events. Politicians blamed local law enforcement for not responding rapidly and appropriately. Others blamed the fact that Cruz had not been properly supervised, or even locked up, because of his behavioural and psychological problems. Few questioned whether these very problems made him unfit to purchase a military-style assault weapon. The National Rifle Association (NRA), for example, had earlier supported President Trump's attempt to overturn an Obama-administration rule that required the Social Security Administration to provide

Table 2.1: Gun deaths in mass killings with more than ten deaths in the US

Year	Incident	Deaths	Injuries	Type of firearm
2018	Stoneman High School	17	17	Semi-automatic rifle
2018	Santa Fe High School	10	14	Shotgun and revolver
2018	Thousand Oaks	13★	8	Semi-automatic pistol and shotgun
2018	Pittsburgh Synagogue	11	7★	Semi-automatic rifle, semi-automatic pistols
2017	Las Vegas	59★	851 (422)	Semi-automatic rifles and revolver
2017	Sutherlands Spring Church	27★	20	Semi-automatic rifle
2016	Orlando Nightclub	50★	53	Semi-automatic rifle and pistol
2015	San Bernardino	16★★	24	Semi-automatic rifles
2015	Umpqua Community College	10★	8	Semi-automatic pistols and revolver
2013	Washington Navy Yard	13★	8	Semi-automatic pistol and shotgun
2012	Sandy Hook Elementary School	28★	2	Semi-automatic rifle and pistol
2012	Aurora	12	70	Semi-automatic rifle, pistol and shotgun

information on mental health disorders during background checks on those attempting to buy guns.

What were some of the major positive responses of leading US politicians to the crime? President Trump proposed that arming and training up to 20 per cent of teachers to deal with terrorists would solve the problem. He also suggested that gun-free schools were a magnet for criminals; rather, guns should be carried in schools as a norm. This line was supported by Texas Lieutenant-Governor Dan Patrick. It also echoed earlier statements by NRA Vice-President Wayne LaPierre, who, after the Sandy Hook Elementary School shooting in December

Year	Incident	Deaths	Injuries	Type of firearm
2009	Binghamton	14★	4	Semi-automatic pistols
2009	Fort Hood	14	33★	Semi-automatic pistol and revolver
2009	Geneva County	11★	6	Semi-automatic rifles, revolver and shotgun
2007	Virginia Tech	33★	23	Semi-automatic pistols
2005	Red Lake	10★	5	Semi-automatic pistols and shotgun
1999	Columbine High School	15★★	24	Semi-automatic rifle, semi-automatic pistol, shotguns
1999	Atlanta	10★	13	Semi-automatic pistols and revolver
1991	Luby's	24★	27	Semi-automatic pistols
1990	GMAC	10★	6	Semi-automatic rifle
1986	Edmund's Post Office	15★	6	Semi-automatic pistols
1984	San Ysidro McDonald's	22★	19	Semi-automatic rifle, pistol, and shotgun
1984	Palm Sunday	10	0	Semi-automatic pistols
1983	Wah Mee	13	1	Semi-automatic pistol and revolver
1982	Wilkes-Barre	13	1	Semi-automatic rifle
1975	Easter Sunday	11	0	Semi-automatic pistols and revolver
1966	University of Texas Tower	18★	31	Rifles, revolver, pistols, and shotgun
1949	Camden	13	3	Semi-automatic pistol

★ Number includes the perpetrator

★★ Number includes both perpetrators

Sources: Pew Center (2017), Mother Jones (2019), Gun Violence Archive (2020)

2012, asserted that 'The only thing that stops a bad guy with a gun is a good guy with a gun'. He went on to claim that federal education budgets can afford to put a police officer in every school. (There was such a guard at Parkland; he remained outside the building during the shooting, saying later he thought that was where the gunman was.)

We cannot, however, simply assume that US politicians are the tools of the NRA and do not reflect public opinion. US citizens' own attitudes towards gun ownership at least in part explain politicians' attitudes. Around two thirds of US citizens say they grew up in, have lived or currently live in a household with guns. Three out of every ten American adults say they own a gun. The largest group of gun owners are white males, of whom 48 per cent own guns, compared to 24 per cent of non-white men and white women, with only 16 per cent of non-white women owning a gun. Gun ownership is highest in rural areas (46 per cent) compared to suburban (28 per cent) and urban (19 per cent). The main reason people say they own a gun is for self-protection, although in rural areas large numbers also give hunting as a reason. Close to 40 per cent of gun owners say they keep a loaded gun accessible when at home, and gun owners are less likely than non-gun owners to think one needs to have taken gun safety courses to own guns or to keep guns locked away. About 75 per cent of gun owners say the right to own a gun is essential (compared to 35 per cent of non-gun owners). About 20 per cent of gun owners belong to the NRA.

About half the population of the US thinks gun violence is a very big problem in their country, varying from 59 per cent of non-gun owners to about 33 per cent of gun owners. Most people (86 per cent) think that the ease of buying illegal guns is the major problem in the US, though 60 per cent also point to the ease of buying guns legally. In fact, 79 per cent of mass shootings in the US involved weapons purchased legally, 19 per cent illegally (2 per cent unknown). So, while a clear majority of the people think gun regulation could be tightened, we cannot be sure that they agree on what those regulations should be.

Senator Marco Rubio claimed that most proposals on gun laws would not have prevented this or other massacres and that instead we should concentrate on the 'violence part'. The Republican governor of Kentucky, Matt Bevin, did suggest some form of regulation – of video games, that he claims desensitize people to the value of human life. The very idea of actually regulating the purchase and use of guns is such anathema that few politicians will even countenance it. But is it really true that gun regulation does not stop or reduce the incidences of such massacres? Does it not reduce the rate of murders, violent crime and suicide? What do the figures tell us?

Let us first look at gun massacres in the US. Table 2.1 lists gun massacres in the US since the end of the Second World War. It is by no means a comprehensive list of all such incidents: it includes only those that resulted in ten or more deaths. We can make a few general points about these incidents of mass slaughter.

First, they all involve semi-automatic weapons, though some additionally involve other sorts of firearms.

Second, all the perpetrators are male (the single exception is San Bernardino, which was a husband and wife terrorist attack). Shootings in general, and mass shootings in particular, are male-dominated. An FBI study found that of 160 'active shooter' incidents in the US between 2000 and 2013 only six (3.8 per cent) involved a female shooter. Of these six incidents, five involved women shooting current or former colleagues at work; the deadliest was a shooting at a post office in Santa Barbara, California, where six people were killed. Other studies using different definitions of shooting incidents find women's involvement similarly low.

Third, around half of the perpetrators (15 out of 29) can be said to have had psychological problems.

In addition to the deaths and injuries recorded in Table 2.1, in the nine years between 2010 and 2018 there were a further 327 deaths and 369 injuries in 76 incidents involving the targeted killing of people, an average of 36 deaths and 41 injuries per year range. Adding the figures from the same years from Table 2.1 tells us that, in the US, between 2010 and 2018, 66 people died in gun massacres each year, while just under 114 were injured.

These death and injury figures are just from gun massacres. They do not include homicides, suicides or accidents, nor other gun-related crime. It is the massacres that make the world headlines (and not even all of them make the international news); such is the number that not all gun-related deaths even make the local news. Quite how many deaths there have been from gun incidents over the years is problematic to calculate, since no official figures on gun incidents or gun-related crime are recorded.

The Gun Violence Archive, set up in 2012, has been collecting data through over 2,500 media, law enforcement, government and commercial services daily, and then separately validating reports. It calculates the number of deaths in the five-year period from 2014 to 2018 as 71,429 (14,286 per year). So, the overall death rate massively exceeds that from massacres. Deaths, of course, are not the only pertinent gun-related figures. In this five-year period, we also find a further 112,947 people injured (22,590 per year). Of these, 11,304 were under the age of 17, and 3,376 were under 11 years old (675 per year). The Gun Violence Archive also logs the number of gun-related incidents in the US in those five years as 276,416: an average of 55,282 per year. (Those incidents include reported events where no deaths or injuries occurred.)

These figures are staggering, especially to those of us who live in comparable developed nations outside the US. To be sure, we can see some similar figures in other countries – failed states, countries ravaged by war or with out-of-control, usually drug-related, organized crime. Depending on the years examined and the source, the US is ranked somewhere between 10th and 20th in the world on firearm-related deaths. Above it in those rankings are states such as El Salvador, Guatemala, Honduras, Jamaica, Swaziland and Venezuela, all notorious for high crime rates, gangland killings, drug issues or, in the case of Swaziland (Eswatini since 2018), continual civil unrest. Some of these countries have a death rate far in excess of that of the US, but they are scarcely comparable in terms of economic development, wealth, crime or civil unrest. The US is generally not considered to be a failed state, nor one whose government cannot control certain regions or parts of cities, as we might think the case in Mexico and some other Central and South American states, or parts of Africa.

Indeed, the figure for guns per inhabitant in the US far exceeds that of any other country in the world. Lower life expectancy, relative to other affluent nations, is not purely due to a high rate of gun-related deaths – the US healthcare and welfare systems have a bigger effect – but it is not an insignificant factor, especially for some social groups.

Guns are a way of life for many US citizens, and the death and injury tolls outlined above are part of that way of life. The Second Amendment to the US Constitution establishes the right to bear arms: 'A well regulated Militia, being necessary to the security of a free State, the right of the people to keep and bear Arms, shall not be infringed'. Does upholding that constitutional right entail that gun regulations be as lax as they are? That is what the debate is really about. It is about regulation – both whether regulations infringe rights and whether stricter regulations would really have a significant effect on those figures.

I will argue that the data strongly suggest that stricter regulations would reduce the gun-related death toll. Let us look at the evidence.

US evidence

Federal restrictions on gun control in the US originate with the Brady Handgun Violence Prevention Act in 1993. It established a federal requirement for a waiting period of up to five days before the transfer of a handgun to a purchaser; during this period a background check would be conducted. From 1998, with the development of the National Instant Criminal Background Check System, administered by the FBI, the federal waiting period was phased out. Many states, however, still require such a waiting period.

State firearm regulations vary a great deal. Some look to provide general oversight of gun owners through permits, registration or licence requirements, and may ban purchase by minors. Other laws attempt to prevent trafficking in guns, ban certain types of arms and restrict the number of firearms that can be sold to individuals. Some laws seek to prevent some people owning guns, including those with criminal records, convictions for felonies or those with a history of mental illness, alcohol or drug problems. Some also insist on a 'cooling-off' period between the initiation and completion of a purchase, to reduce impulse buys. These variations allow us to assess whether tighter regulations have any measurable effect on gun violence.

Gun crime

The US has higher rates of both fatal and non-fatal violent crime than virtually all other countries in the developed world; the majority of these crimes involve firearms; the US has a higher rate of gun ownership than most other developed nations. Many people conclude, accordingly, that gun ownership is a major cause of this violence. They assume that stricter gun laws will reduce violent crime and murder rates. That conclusion is controversial. Of course, in the public debate in the US, claiming that ready access to guns has anything whatsoever to do with crime will always be controversial. The NRA and other radical groups ensure that reasoned debate in public will always be shouted down.

Nevertheless, the academic literature does not uniformly support the conclusion that stricter regulations will reduce crime. A number of studies suggests otherwise. I choose my evidence from careful reviews and meta-analyses, and one or two of the most carefully argued and more sceptical pieces. After all, cross-country comparison, of the sort we see on page 35, has the problem that different countries vary in a greater number of ways than gun ownership. They have different welfare systems, different levels of inequality, different laws, different ways of organizing the police and judicial systems, as well as more difficult-to-categorize cultural facts. And, of course, one cultural fact is that many US citizens defend the right to bear arms and own guns. Even though statistical analysis can control for many of these factors in various ways, some argue that the best comparisons have to be within-country comparisons. These are the studies that suggest that gun control laws have little effect on gun-related crime.

At first sight, this might seem surprising, given just how much gun crime there is in the US compared to other countries. However, when we compare variation in gun control laws across US states with variation across countries, we see that in fact there is, relatively speaking, little variation across US states. Moreover, of course, while there are rules against trafficking some types of firearms interstate, those involved in crime are not likely to be much deterred. Guns are transportable across state lines and into municipalities. So we might expect little variation in gun crime.

What the evidence does show is that, while the majority of the different regulations seems to have little impact on rates of gun violence, requiring a gun licence and banning alcoholics from purchasing guns seems to reduce homicide and robbery rates.

Banning the sale of guns to those with a criminal record and those deemed mentally ill also seems to reduce assault rates. Banning gun purchase by those with a criminal record seems to reduce robbery rates. The conclusion is fairly clear. Stricter regulations do have an effect, but only a small one – when the change in regulations is small. For more radical shifts, more radical changes in regulations would be required. The relevant evidence is the differences between US gun laws and regulation elsewhere and the differences in rates of gun crime inside and outside the US.

Suicide

In a survey of 36 wealthy nations, the US had not only the highest overall firearm mortality rate, but the highest proportion of suicides by firearm. Each year in the US, guns are used for more suicides than homicides. While some studies find no correlation between suicide rates and stricter gun control, they tend to use cross-sectional data and simple correlational analysis and do not consider the nature of stricter gun laws. Some firearm regulations are more pertinent to suicide prevention than others. Requiring permits and cooling-off periods may prevent impulse buys, and prohibiting some categories of persons such as those with psychological, drug or alcohol problems may also have an effect. Most analyses of the relationship between regulation and suicide find a strong link between suicide rates and gun regulation in the US. One of the most comprehensive studies, by Antonio Andrés and Katherine Hempstead finds:

> gun control measures do not affect all age groups identically ... a ban on firearm purchases by minors affects suicides particularly among younger males, while restrictions on permits and waiting period requirements have a more deterrent effect for older males.

This study also finds that stricter regulations for those with drug and alcohol problems reduce suicide rates, but differently across different age groups. The authors conclude that restricting access to firearms can have a significant effect on male suicide rates.

Academics, politicians, the media and the public might argue about the real effects of gun culture on mortality and injury rates; the one sector that has absolutely no doubt is the insurance industry. Estimates give the mark-up for the high death rate from all forms of firearm death on a $1,000 20-year term insurance starting at age 25 of about 10 per cent for the population as a whole. This varies from a low 4.5 per cent for white females to a high of about 19 per cent for black males.

International comparisons

Table 2.2 orders guns per 100,000 population for the 40 countries with the most guns per 100,000. The figures are taken from different sources with varying degrees of accuracy, so may not be strictly comparable. Some war-torn countries that do not appear in the table might have more guns, but no reliable estimates can be made. We might also note that these are guns per head of civilians, not military; in some countries, where there is compulsory civilian service in the military, the guns-per-head figure does not include the weapons that civilians are required to keep as members of the military reserve and which would only be used during military service. Nevertheless, despite the approximate nature of the numbers, we can see that the US easily outstrips all other countries in the world in the number of guns per head of population. It has almost four times as many guns per head of population as the next highest country, Serbia.

Table 2.2 also shows approximate death rates. Again, the figures are not strictly comparable, as they are less reliable in some countries than others, and they cover different time periods. Nevertheless, they clearly show that the numbers of guns per 100,000 do not directly correlate with the death rate by firearm per 100,000. Way down the table we find Venezuela and Honduras with a tenth or less of the gun ownership of the US, but a death rate almost six times higher. Guatemala also has a notably high death rate. Other countries that do not appear in the table, since they are not in the top 40 for gun ownership, but whose death rate by firearm exceeds that of the US, include Columbia, El Salvador, Jamaica and Swaziland (Eswatini).

Table 2.2: Guns per 100,000 people

Country	Guns per 100,000	Approximate death rate
United States	121	12
Serbia	38	3.5
Cyprus	36	2
Uruguay	32	12
Norway	32	1.75
Austria	31	3
Germany	31	1
Iceland	31	1
New Zealand	30	1
Finland	28	2
Canada	25	2
Kuwait	25	0.33
Switzerland	24	3
Montenegro	23	9
Greece	23	1.5
Panama	22	15
Sweden	21	1.5
Qatar	19	0.15
Latvia	19	1.5
Peru	19	5.5
Paraguay	17	7.75
Czech Republic	16	2
Spain	16	0.5
Luxembourg	15	1.25
Mexico	15	7.5
France	15	3
Croatia	15	2.5
Australia	14	1
Slovenia	14	2.75
Guatemala	13	34
South Africa	12	8.5
Denmark	12	1
Italy	12	1.25
Venezuela	11	60
Chile	10	2.4
Honduras	11	60
Estonia	9	2.67
Argentina	9	7
Brazil	9	22

Sources: GunPolicy.org (2020) and Vox (2017)

Of course, gun ownership per se is not going to correlate perfectly with deaths by guns. Disproportionately higher death rates are inevitable in failed states, those torn by civil strife or those with areas that are essentially outside government control – no-go areas controlled by gangs and so on. The countries to compare to the US are those with similarly powerful states, with strong legal systems and the rule of law. We can see that a number of developed industrial nations have gun ownership rates near the top of the table – Cyprus, Norway, Austria, Germany, Iceland, New Zealand, Finland and Canada – yet they all have some of the lowest rates of death by firearm. This suggests that the cause of high death rates is not gun ownership in itself, but something about the nature of the countries or their gun regulation.

Are the high mortality and injury rates from gun-related incidents simply part of US culture? For some, the answer is yes. High gun ownership and acceptance of the high casualty rates are what it means to be part of the culture. We have seen that many Americans accept and defend high gun ownership, and we can point to the Second Amendment to say that this culture has been part of the American way of life for over two centuries.

Yet we can hardly explain the high number of gun incidents by the culture itself, when we also understand it to be part of that culture. We can note, too, wide variations in both ownership and incidents across communities that show that the culture is far from uniform. More importantly, as we shall see below, we find that changing the regulatory framework in the US has had a clear impact on the number of gun-related incidents, suggesting that the regulatory framework is at least part of the story. Indeed, regulation frames culture to some extent; if we wanted to change the gun culture of the US, we could only achieve that through changing the regulatory framework. It is true that changing gun regulations might not be sufficient to reduce gun-related violence in the US to levels seen in comparable countries, but it is surely a necessary component. Let us compare the gun regulation in those countries comparable to the US.

Near the top of Table 2.2, with gun ownership at 25 or more per 100,000 of population, we have a number of Western industrial or post-industrial nations that are similar to the US in terms of political culture: Cyprus, Norway, Austria, Germany,

Iceland, New Zealand, Finland and Canada. All of them have a low death rate per 100,000 of the population. We can also note Uruguay, whose death rate through guns is similar to the US, though its gun ownership is much lower. That in itself shows that guns per se are not the simple cause of rate of deaths by firearms – all things being equal, though, we must conclude that the higher the percentage of gun ownership, the higher the death rate.

To gain insight into death rates, we need to view gun regulation in the comparator countries alongside regulation in the US. Table 2.3 summarizes the regulatory processes of the eight comparator nations and the US. The US is the only country where people have a right to bear arms. As we have seen, while regulation of all forms of firearms varies from state to state in the US, only automatic firearms are subject to laws that approach those of the comparator nations. There is no registration of firearm ownership in the US, and while dealers are required to keep a register of all sales, private sales are allowed, with no

Table 2.3: Summary of weapon type regulations

Country	Auto	Semi-auto	Handguns	Long guns	Limits
US	Regulated	Yes	Yes	Yes	No
Cyprus	No	Special permit	Special permit	Regulated	Yes
Norway	Regulated	Regulated	Regulated	Regulated	Yes
Austria	No	Special permit	Special permit	Regulated	Yes
Germany	No	Special permit	Special permit	Regulated	One only
Iceland	Regulated	Regulated	Regulated	Regulated	No
New Zealand	No*	No*	Regulated	Regulated	No
Finland	No	Special permit	Regulated	Regulated	10
Canada	No *	Regulated	Regulated	Regulated	No

Yes = permitted

No = not permitted

* = permitted in special circumstances

Sources: GunPolicy.org (2020), Vox (2017) and Tenorio et al (2016)

official registration or checking process in place. Some states require a permit to allow open and/or concealed carrying of guns, others do not. Furthermore, the checks that are in place when purchasing a gun (which again vary from state to state) tend to be cursory. Meanwhile, the penalty for illegal possession of a gun in the US is ten years, which is as tough a sentence as anywhere in the world.

All the other countries have much more restrictive gun laws than the US. In all of them a licence is required in order to own a gun, and for such a licence to be granted a reason for gun ownership must be provided. The precise reasons that are acceptable vary slightly from country to country, but generally include hunting, target shooting, being a gun collector, reasons of employment and personal protection or security. (In New Zealand, owning a firearm for self-defence is specifically excluded and prohibited, while no reason needs to be provided for the purchase of standard hunting or shooting firearms.)[1]

All eight countries carry out systematic and extensive background checks on people who want to own guns. The applicants must pass a background check that generally demands a clear history on mental health, criminality and, in many countries (for example, Cyprus, Canada and New Zealand), no record of domestic violence. In some countries (such as Germany), alcohol or drug addiction is a reason for refusing a licence. In Cyprus, Canada and New Zealand, third-party references for good character are also required. In New Zealand, the licensing authority will also conduct interviews with the applicant's spouse, partner or next of kin. Private sales of weapons are banned in most of the countries (Cyprus allows them, but they must all be registered with the regulatory authority). All the countries keep official records of gun ownership, though whether these are held by national or state agencies varies (in New Zealand, hunting or shooting weapons are excluded). Gun dealers must keep records of all sales with the details of the purchasers. All the countries (except Finland) require applicants to have taken a theoretical or practical training course, though how intensive those courses actually are varies widely.

In most of the eight countries the open or concealed carrying of weapons is banned or only allowed by permit under exceptional circumstances. The ages at which people may legally purchase guns varies, but is generally set at 18, or 21 for some categories of firearms (in some countries, those under that age can own guns with parental permission and guidance). The penalties for illegal possession vary from three months' imprisonment in Norway to up to ten years in several countries. And, as we see in the final column of Table 2.3, the limits on the number of weapons a person can own vary from country to country.

We can surmise, therefore, that while the rate of gun ownership per 100,000 is greater in the US than its comparator countries, it is not this fact alone that causes the much higher gun incident and death rates. The regulatory framework is important. Of course, if the laws do the job that they are designed for, they will affect the rate of gun ownership, since they ought to keep legal weapons out of the hands of the mentally disturbed, those with a criminal record and those who have committed domestic violence. They will also surely reduce the number of people with access to semi-automatic assault firearms – the favoured weapons of those who have committed mass atrocities such as the one that opened this chapter. The much stricter regulation of automatic and semi-automatic weapons and handguns is perhaps one of the most important factors. The stricter background checks on mental health help reduce both mass shooting and suicide, while criminal record checks help reduce the amount of gun-related crime and, arguably, violent crime in general. Making registration more difficult also reduces impulse buys and requires that people have valid reasons to buy not only weapons in general, but a gun that fits the activity they claim they want it for. On the other hand, the severity of punishment for illegal possession – where the US is the most draconian – seems to have no effect.

This claim that tighter regulation seems to reduce gun-related death by a considerable amount is confirmed by a systematic review, published in 2016, of the academic evidence. This study, by Julian Santaella-Tenorio, Magdalena Cerdá, Andrés Villaveces and Sandro Galea, examines evidence from 130 primary studies of the effects on regulations on gun violence. The authors defined arms-related legislation as any regulations or restrictions on the use, sale, ownership or storage of firearms.

Their definition includes within it the banning of ownership of certain types of weapons, registration of weapons and also the use of voluntary rendition of firearms through buyback programmes. This systematic review suggests that, while it is difficult to pinpoint the precise regulations that reduce firearm deaths, the simultaneous implementation of multiple restrictions on the purchase and use of guns has a major effect on gun violence, including the death rate. The features that are associated with lower gun violence include banning automatic weapons and restricting the sale of semi-automatic weapons and handguns, implementing background checks and requiring people to get permits. Registering all sales has not been shown to be important, but this is probably because there is so little variance in that practice. Of course, both registration and background check processes vary in how efficiently they are conducted.

The authors conclude that there is compelling evidence of specific laws reducing the rate of firearm deaths. Studies show that the quality of systems used in background checks is vital. As an example of such a background check, confirming whether there is a restraining order on a potential purchaser is associated with a reduction in the rate of murders of female partners. Meanwhile, checking felony prosecution is associated with a lower unintentional death rate of children through firearm discharge. The first provides the obvious mechanism for the reduction in gun deaths. Violent men with access to guns are more likely to kill their partners by using a gun than if that access is restricted. The second mechanism is less obvious. However, felony prosecutions are suggestive of a less organized attitude to life that might extend to care over weapons. We know that laws governing safe storage are also associated with lower rates of unintentional deaths and intimate partner homicides. Where it is less easy to access a gun, it is less likely that a gun will be used or go off accidently. Similarly, a violent person might, in a fit of anger, pick up a gun that is handy and use it against their partner. If they had to fetch the gun from a locked cupboard and then load it, killing in the heat of the moment is no longer possible.

The study also looks at cases where the regulations have been relaxed. In 2007, the state of Missouri repealed the requirement to obtain a permit for purchasing a firearm, and the homicide rate subsequently increased by 25 per cent.

We would expect that mental health checks would have a significant effect on the suicide rate by firearm, although we might doubt whether that reduction would affect the underlying suicide rate, due to substitution effects. Shooting is a preferred suicide method for men with access to guns, and is relatively easy and successful in comparison to other methods. The suicidal will often find a way of committing suicide whether or not they have access to guns. However, substitution methods ought to lead to a reduction in overall suicide rates, since the success rate of would-be suicides is greater by firearm than other methods. One study showed that fatality rates for suicide in the north-eastern US was 91 per cent for firearms, but 84 per cent for drowning, 82 per cent for hanging and only 14 per cent for poisoning with drugs. The last is the preferred method used by about three quarters of those attempting suicide – and the vast majority of people who survive a suicide attempt do not later die by suicide. Mental health checks should also reduce the incidence of mass shootings, because of the strong correlation between underlying psychological problems and mass shooters.

Deaths and injuries through firearm use fall into different categories, which are governed by separate types of mechanism. This explains why multiple regulatory methods are highly correlated with lower levels of gun incidents: some regulations affect some categories more than others. The broad ambit of the regulatory framework is thus important to catch as many categories as possible in its net.

Australia: a case study

Australia provides a case study that social scientists sometimes call a natural experiment. Within 12 days of the Port Arthur mass killings in Tasmania on 28–9 April 1996, when 35 people were shot dead and 18 wounded, the federal and state governments of Australia agreed to enact uniform gun control laws. These were progressively enacted between June 1996 and August 1998. Before then, Australia had, in international terms, relatively relaxed gun laws (though much stricter than the US). Until

1996 all gun legislation in Australia was enacted by the states and territories. Legal requirements varied: Tasmania and Queensland had no requirement for licensing or registration of firearms, some states required registration for handguns only, others also required registration of 'long guns' (rifles and shotguns). After the Port Arthur massacre in 1996, and again after a shooting at Monash University in 2002, federal legislation was enacted. Its centrepiece was the National Firearms Agreement (1996). This placed strict controls on semi-automatic and fully automatic weapons, allowing only licensed individuals to own them and excluding personal protection as a legitimate purpose. As part of that legislation, over 650,000 firearms were bought back by the government (at a cost averaging around $320 per gun).

Australia thus provides a nice natural experiment where we can compare gun incidents of all types before and after significantly stricter gun regulation. The simple figures seem straightforward. The decline in total firearm deaths and decline in total firearm suicides both accelerated after the introduction of gun laws in 1996. In all forms it decreased by an average of 1 per cent before the introduction of gun laws but decreased by an average of 4.4 per cent after their introduction. Homicides overall remained at about the same rate for many years before the introduction of gun laws, but decreased by about 3.3 per cent per annum afterwards.

There does appear to be some substitution effects for suicides – that is, once guns are not available, people choose other methods – but this is difficult to judge precisely. The annual suicide rate is determined by many other factors, and the long-term trends seem to suggest an overall reduction independent of any firearm effects.

Alongside the new federal laws which affect all of Australia, there were changes in state laws, which also constitute natural experiments. For example, in 1988 Victoria had introduced stricter regulation of semi-automatic 'longarms' (rifles) following a mass shooting, the Hoddle and Queen Street massacre of 15 people in 1987. Victoria also passed its own Firearms Act in 1996 alongside the federal legislation in response to the Port Arthur massacre. For a decade prior to 1987 the observed rate of firearm-related deaths in both Victoria and Australia as a whole remained relatively flat. In 1987 the rate in Victoria was higher than that for Australia as whole (in part because of the Hoddle and Queen Street massacre). Subsequently, from 1987 to 1996, the rate of firearm deaths for Victoria was below that of the rest of Australia. The national rate increased in 1996 because of Tasmania's Port Arthur massacre, but it then dropped quickly to match that of Victoria from 1997 onwards. Radical regulatory reforms appear to have achieved dramatic reductions in overall firearm-related deaths and particularly suicides by firearms.

The right to buy and regulation

In part this chapter is designed to show that government regulation has a large effect upon outcomes. Gun legislation is a good example for demonstrating how government regulations affect outcomes, since the issue is relatively straightforward, both in terms of regulatory frameworks and the outcome being assessed – number of deaths and injuries from gun-related incidents. It is also a good example because the US is such a palpable outlier from other comparable countries. We can see the dramatic difference that stricter regulations have made to deaths and injuries in other countries in comparison to the US. Since some people claim, in the face of this overwhelming evidence, that there are also cultural differences between the US and other countries that might explain why it is an outlier, we can also look at evidence in the US. Here again, it shows that stricter regulation in some states has an effect; and when legislation was relaxed in Missouri, the homicide rate increased. These effects are small, but this is something we should expect, given that it is easy (and legal) to take guns across state boundaries. Thus we show, clearly, that government regulation matters. Of course, government has always believed that or it would not bother to regulate in the first place.

The right to buy guns, based on the Constitution's Second Amendment, is so entrenched in the psyche of so many US citizens that the very idea of regulating their sale already seems to be a fundamental attack on the American way of life. Maybe it is. However, the debate over regulation in the US is rarely publicly aired, since any attempt to discuss regulation is overwhelmed by the NRA and media into turning it into a debate about banning guns. There is no serious proposal from any politician, lobby or citizen group, as far as I am aware, about banning guns, just regulating their sale. There are many options in such regulations, as I have discussed in this chapter.

However, even if any form of gun regulation is anathema to the citizens of the US and to their governments based on the constitutional right to bear arms, then they must take full responsibility for the consequences of this right. They must say in response not only to the massacres of their children in schools and universities, of their colleagues and friends in their workplaces, but also to the murders, suicides and accidents that cause such a massive death toll, that these are part and parcel of the American way of life. If US citizens and their rulers want to defend the current gun laws and the right to bear arms, including assault weapons, then they have to take responsibility for all of these outcomes. Outcomes that we know, statistically, result from the regulations that currently exist. We know the correlation and we have a pretty good idea of the causal mechanisms that lead from those rights to the death rate.

We do not have to ban gun ownership. Gun ownership exists in various forms all over the world. Regulations, such as stricter background checks, mental health assessments, restricting the purchase of automatic weapons and so on, are likely to reduce the death toll, particularly from massacres. These are rules that could be put in place and enforced. We know from the Australian 'natural experiment' what a huge difference tightening up gun laws makes. The evidence is clear.

Final word

Those who want to defend lax gun regulations should stand up and take responsibility for what they believe in. They believe in the right to bear guns, to own assault weapons. They believe gun control infringes those rights. They believe those rights are worth the ensuing carnage: the massacres, the murders, the suicides, the accidents. They need to admit that fact, and publicly defend it.

3

Obesity

There is no doubt that, in the developed world, people, by various measures, are healthier than they have ever been. Mortality and morbidity rates have fallen over the past century or more, notwithstanding occasional blips when crises such as war or economic depression have halted or temporarily reversed gains. The crude death rate in the US, for example, has fallen from around 1 per cent to about 0.8 per cent since the 1940s, but the age-adjusted rate has fallen much more quickly. People on average live longer, since fewer people die young.

This trend is a global phenomenon; and the biggest falls in death rates have occurred in countries with the fastest economic growth rates. We know that mortality and morbidity rates are correlated with per capita gross domestic product (GDP), although the quite large variation across countries shows that other factors are also important. We know, too, that mortality and morbidity rates vary across social classes, with the rich living longer and, on average, having better health than poorer people. We can further note that, while this increase in the health of the world's population is enhanced by better health *care* (that is, the provision of medical services), the major cause is healthier lifestyles due to better food, water and living conditions.

Despite this good news for people's health, there is growing concern in the developed world about increasing obesity among the population. This was first brought to public attention by health professionals – the World Health Organization was a major player in publicizing the issue – but it is increasingly discussed by politicians, commentators and the public.

The issue has been described as a crisis, and obesity as an epidemic. These rhetorical flourishes are to be expected when an issue is first brought to public attention. In themselves, they are not very helpful descriptions. The scale of the obesity crisis is highly contested, with some people suggesting we should not concern ourselves with body shape. The manner in which it is discussed also varies cross-nationally. In the UK, for example, the costs to the taxpayer-funded NHS are a concern. Obesity therefore becomes a public issue, since those not suffering health problems due to excess weight subsidize the health costs of those who are. In countries with less socialized medicine, the interpersonal or social costs of weight problems are normally couched only in terms of how they affect production and hence economic growth. In that sense, obesity is seen as a concern of the community, since the obesity of some individuals limits the prosperity of all.

Even if people's obesity affected no one but themselves, however, it is perfectly reasonable for the community to be concerned about the body shape of individuals, especially if public policy is implicated in those personal problems. If each individual's body shape was entirely within their own control, then perhaps others should keep away from the issue. But it is not. Genetic and historical factors are implicated in how one's body responds to its food intake and to exercise. And, more importantly as far as I am concerned in this book, food manufacturers deliberately add sugar, sweeteners, fats and salt to food, because in doing so they appeal to our taste buds – and can, indeed, form an addiction. Indeed, modern ultra-processed food has few if any nutrients that sustain us; rather, it is manufactured using chemicals designed to stimulate dopamine production in the brain to make the consumer crave more of the product. We know that these additives affect the body shape of consumers, and they are outside their control. People are being manipulated by food manufacturers, and government is doing nothing to protect people from that exploitation.

Obesity is particularly interesting in the context of this book, since it has long been considered that individuals should take personal responsibility for their weight and body shape. It is also a fraught issue, since body shape is something that is deeply personal; fat shaming through verbal abuse – in the playground, on television and increasingly through social media – is itself a problem. Large size might be a lifestyle choice. Being overweight does not necessarily entail that one is unhealthy (although, as we shall see, at population level there is a correlation between body shape and health). In fact, the 'ideal body shape' shifts to some extent with fashion. In the past, the poor were thin and the rich fat: larger body shape was a mark of high status. So what we see as a problem again depends, at least in part, upon social norms.

It is perhaps because so many people take it for granted that one's weight and body shape are one's personal responsibility that a large part of the discussion about obesity is directed at children. Children are not expected to take full responsibility for their health and, while parents are expected to be aware of health issues for children, looking after child welfare where parents fail is commonly more accepted by the general population. So the child obesity crisis is often the topic of discussion – with the background knowledge, among health professionals at least, that body shape as a child is highly correlated with body shape as an adult.

We might be more concerned with childhood than adult obesity for a number of reasons. One is that we do not consider children to be responsible; they are not rational consumers, so they need greater protection. The second is the strong correlation between childhood weight issues and major obesity problems later in life. I think the first reason is a poor one. Part of the argument of this book is that we cannot expect individual people to be responsible for the general trends in society, of which their own behaviour is a part. We can give them relative responsibility, relative to other people like them in the relevant respects, but that is all. Second, and particularly pertinent to weight issues, is that we naturally fall into certain sorts of behaviours. Evolution has set us up to enjoy sweet, salty and fatty foods. When food is scarce, those evolutionarily induced tastes are good for our general health. Given how we have developed food production in the market economy, they are bad. We cannot expect people to take responsibility for these evolutionarily developed tastes. We should be able to expect our governments, and society, to take responsibility for regulating, since we know we all have these evolutionarily developed tastes.

What is obesity?

Obese simply means being grossly overweight. Its official definition relates to having a body mass index (BMI) of 30 or higher. BMI is calculated by dividing a person's weight in kilograms by their height in metres squared. Generally speaking, a BMI of 25 or over is considered overweight, 30 or over obese. If someone's BMI is below 18.5, they are considered to be underweight. Originally the BMI scale was used by epidemiologists to analyze trends in public heath, but it has come to be used as a common tool in medical practice. This shift in use is relevant to my argument in this book. As a measure of individual health or obesity, the BMI scale is fairly crude. Individuals have different characteristics in terms of bone structure, muscles and where their fat is stored – in short, body shape – which have implications for whether careful medical assessment will consider them to be overweight. For example, BMI is not the most accurate measure of abdominal obesity (magnetic resource imaging or dual energy x-ray absorptiometry are better). So, at the individual level, BMI is perhaps useful as a starting point to examine individual health, but not as an end point. A person who calculates that their own BMI is, say, 27, might want to take advice on whether they are overweight; a specialist might confirm that they are, or they might say that, given their body shape and muscular development, they need have no concerns over their weight.

BMI is not, however, a crude instrument when it comes to the purpose it was originally designed for. It usefully measures how a population overall, and subgroups within it, is faring with regard to weight issues. Individual variation in body size – those aspects of body shape that matter for the evaluation of individual health – washes out in the general analysis. It is true that certain types of people – for example, different ethnicities or age groups – might, as types, be marked by differences in BMI measures which have no implications for the relative health of those types. We discovered this very fact, that 'healthy BMI' differs across types of people, precisely by measuring BMI, coding by type and correlating with the overall health of those different types.

People do not readily understand why a measure such as BMI is a crude device at the individual level, but instructive when used at the population level. Measures which are applied to types of people can be very accurate for their purpose with regard to those types, but not so useful when applied to particular individuals. Government policy needs to be directed at types of people rather than individuals as such, yet it is also desirable that public servants on the front line – so-called 'street-level bureaucrats' – should have discretion as to which policies should be applied to individual cases and how this should be done. BMI is a useful tool for policy makers as they examine trends in society, but should only be a starting point for doctors and health professionals when they are dealing with individual people.

Body-shape problems and health

We have seen that obesity is rather a complex issue. Body shape is not only a health issue, but also a social one. Social mores suggest that some types of body shape are preferable, or better, or more acceptable, than others. There does seem to be some evolutionary (that is, not contingent) aspect to 'ideal body shape' – such as the appeal of 'child-bearing hips' in women – that transcends cultural differences, as do some features of good health reflected in appearance, such as symmetrical facial features in both men and women. Beyond these aspects, though, what society views as ideal body size varies cross-culturally. In Western society over the last century, the ideal body shape for women demands slimness, though recently a larger posterior has come into fashion. Social pressures to achieve the 'right' body shape, especially for women, cause all sorts of psychological problems; the flip side of the obesity problem is eating disorders such as anorexia nervosa.

Much of the debate over the 'obesity epidemic' in modern societies is conducted in terms of health issues and the costs to society of those health issues – loss of production, strains on the healthcare system, and so on. But poor health is an aspect of individual welfare, and to the extent that we care about human well-being and happiness we ought to care about the effects of body size on individuals in terms of both physical and mental health. However, we also believe that, generally speaking, individuals are and should remain the privileged authority on their own well-being. There is nothing puzzling about someone choosing to indulge in an activity they enjoy, even if it poses a risk to their health and life expectancy. While we might want to regulate risky sports activities – or at least encourage those indulging in them to pay for the risks through insurance and provide regulation of those providing equipment and facilities for safety and care – some of the enjoyment of such activities depends on the risk, and there is nothing wrong with people taking risks in order to enjoy their lives. Similarly, it is not irrational to accept that the way one eats and drinks is likely to reduce one's life expectancy by, say, two years yet still want to eat that way. Surely it is better to be relatively happy for 78 years than relatively miserable for 80.

In other words, any proposal to regulate what people eat is already seemingly challenging the privilege that people have with regard to choices about their own lifestyle. But not all types of regulation impact on choice in the same way. For example, a national diet plan, where everyone would eat the same dish at the same time, every day of the week, affects choice in a completely different way from a ban on the injection of water into chickens that are to be frozen and sold. It is true, of course, that regulating food production, perhaps banning some type of force feeding of animals, will have an impact on the price of meat, meaning that some people could not eat meat so often. But even that kind of regulation is not of the same order as implementing a national diet plan.

Regulating the amount of sugar, or salt, or other ingredients in manufactured food, either by directly limiting the additives or through high taxation of excess amounts of such additives, would not take away general freedom of choice over food. Of course, it would mean that food with that amount of additives would not be available – but then, manufactured food with fewer additives is not available currently for most people. Regulation therefore would not reduce choice, but rather change choice. While it is plausible to suggest that reducing the range of choice reduces freedom, it is less plausible to claim that changing the array of options does so. Indeed, if the changes lead to high-quality options then it is plausible to suggest that our freedom has increased. If some of the additives that are known to have universal appeal to people were regulated, manufacturers might need to distinguish their products in other ways in order to generate appeal. After all, gourmets tend to think that manufactured and processed food is dull and boring precisely because to the educated palate – the palate that tries many different sorts of food – highly processed foods all tend to taste the same.

Liberty might be restricted if the prices of such products were to increase, either because people would not be able to buy so much food or, if they did, they would not be able to afford so many other goods. That is correct: liberty would be affected. If one runs that argument against intervening in markets, however, one also ought to run another argument alongside it. Perfect markets are usually considered to be efficient when the price has been reduced to such an extent that the marginal (or last) good produced by the firm brings it no profit. Excess profits show that the market is not efficient. One way of regulating markets would be a higher tax on excessive profits – that would give firms incentives to reduce their prices to keep profits within reasonable limits. By the argument above, that would also increase liberty. Either way we have regulation.

However, what we do see in functioning markets today is how firms respond to regulations. If they were forced to reduce the salts, sugar and fats in their products, they would certainly experiment to see how they could produce better and cheaper products than their rivals. Or they might simply reduce portion size. We cannot just assume that such regulations will increase price in a manner that will materially affect individual liberty even as it increases individual welfare.

Would the individual enjoyment of products change if salts, sugars and fats were reduced? Perhaps. After all, food manufacturers augment their products with large amounts of sugar and salt precisely because their experiments and market research demonstrate that people prefer manufactured food with such quantities of additives. They would undoubtedly experiment to see what people liked without so many additions, and our taste buds would adapt. After all, these human preferences for what we currently face have been distorted by factors at play in the context of modern society.

Despite my claim that we have a very good idea about how we can improve human welfare through regulation of food manufacture, the obesity issue is more complex to consider in terms of regulation than, say, gun control. Few people would claim that mass murders or the high rate of murders, accidental death, suicides and injuries caused by guns are not a problem; there is more dispute about body size. In the next sections I will review the evidence that we know, by and large, the determinants of the body-shape and obesity problems of modern society. That is, we know why growing numbers of people have high BMI scores, including those deemed obese by that measure. We can therefore introduce regulations to control both the level and the distribution of body-shape problems in society. Because we know these facts, the responsibility for both the level and the distribution of weight problems in society lies at the feet of government and not individuals. Following a discussion of that evidence, I will return to some of the problematic issues concerning responsibility, fat shaming and individual liberty.

Is there a crisis of obesity?

Simple descriptive statistics suggest that people being overweight and obesity are immediate and growing problems. In the US their rapid rise began in the late 1970s. Between 1960 and 1980, obesity increased by around 1.3 per cent per annum to encompass around 15 per cent of the population. Since then, obesity has more than doubled to around 35 per cent of the population, with an annual rate of increase of around 4.7 per cent. Grade III obesity (BMI in excess of 40) has grown even more rapidly. Conditions associated with obesity – type 2 diabetes, various forms of cancer (endometrial, postmenopausal breast, kidney and colon cancers), heart disease, musculoskeletal disorders, sleep apnoea and gallbladder problems – together account for around 400,000 deaths per annum in the US; only tobacco is deadlier.

Similarly, in Australia, obesity rates have risen sharply: around 30 per cent of the population are now deemed to be obese, rising from 18 per cent in the mid-1990s. Around two thirds of the population are either overweight or obese. One in four Australian children is overweight, with 7 per cent of children considered obese. The geographical distribution of body-shape problems shows that inner cities and outer regional and remote areas are the worst affected, largely explained by social class divisions. Weight problems are also greater in Indigenous communities than in the settler population. Evidence also shows that the biggest increases in weight occur within newly arrived immigrant communities, where the change in diet and lifestyle has dramatic effects. Immigrant communities are also more likely to suffer type 2 diabetes at any level of weight gain than second-generation settlers. As in the US, type 2 diabetes is increasing at a rate of around 40 per cent per annum.

We see a similar picture in the UK, with about 28 per cent of the population deemed to be obese, and a further 35 per cent overweight. Child obesity, too, is rising: around 17 per cent are obese and a further 15 per cent overweight. Studies in the UK suggest obesity reduces life expectancy on average by about three years; life expectancy for those with a BMI over 40, though, is reduced by 8–10 years. The costs of obesity to the NHS have been calculated at around £5 billion per annum, and the costs to the economy at around £27 billion.

We can also see how weight affects health by looking at relative expenditure on health per person. The average expenditure on health for each obese person is about 38 per cent higher than for those who are not obese. A degree of scepticism about some of the claims for the costs of obesity may perhaps be justified. It has been suggested, for example, that in socialized medical systems there is no extra cost overall for obese people: while their annual bills are higher, their life expectancy is low enough to entail that their lifetime health expenditure is no greater than for the non-obese. The rise in type 2 diabetes may be attributed in part to increased diagnoses rather than a rise in the underlying level of disease alone. Nevertheless, the raw figures are enough to demonstrate that obesity is a modern issue, since obesity rates have risen since the early 1980s, and so steeply that one can hardly deny it is a problem, even if one wishes to avoid the drama of calling it a crisis.

The causes of the increase in obesity

There is no single cause of the increase in obesity in society. We know that obesity in adulthood is directly related to childhood obesity, but not all adults who become obese were so as children. However, we do know that the start of the big increase in obesity in the Western world occurred in the late 1970s to early 1980s. So, whatever the cause of that increasing trend, it is something that happened structurally at that time.

Before the 1980s, people had weight problems; some were obese. Being overweight was discussed in health circles, and there were plenty of commercially promoted diet plans, slimming groups and so on. But the 1980s saw a qualitative change in the extent of body-shape problems. That alone should tell us that we cannot simply blame individuals and hold them entirely responsible for their weight, unless we want to claim that people suddenly became irresponsible at that particular time. So what has happened since the 1970s to cause the increase in obesity?

Two main factors emerge from the scientific evidence: the food we eat and the exercise we take. The latter is less well documented than the former, but most observers agree that children spend less time playing out of doors and more time watching television and using computers than in the past (it is worth noting, though, that children spending too long reading books was similarly complained of in earlier generations). Children are less likely to walk or cycle to school, while modern workplaces are generally more sedentary than in the past, and people are more likely to commute by car than cycle, walk or use public transport (which also usually means we walk further).

The role of sugar

There is very strong evidence that sugar-sweetened beverages (SSBs) are associated with high calorific intake. This association does not simply derive from the fact that SSBs are themselves high in calories; people, notably children and adolescents, who consume them frequently are also likely to consume greater quantities of solid food with higher calorific content. We also see replacement effects: people drinking SSBs are less likely to drink water and milk, and have a lower intake of fresh fruit. A study has shown that those who consume the most SSBs have the highest risks of developing type 2 diabetes. While this study only compares the risk between the highest and lowest consumers, we can surmise that those in between will have 'in-between' effects. Certainly, it demonstrates the harmful effects of such sugars.

The sugars that have been shown to have an effect on obesity are 'free sugars' – those that are added to food along with a high intake of some naturally occurring sugars found in honey, syrup and fruits. Reducing the intake of such sugars in controlled cases has been demonstrated to reduce body weight in adults, albeit by small amounts. Any reduction in sugar has an effect upon body weight.

While it was once thought that high sugar consumption is associated with diabetes and increased risks of cardiovascular disease only through weight gain, recent evidence suggests that excess sugar consumption has a direct effect on chronic illnesses including diabetes mellitus, liver cirrhosis and dementia. The mechanism that causes this is so far unknown, but epidemiological study suggests the effect is also direct. Systematic review and meta-analysis demonstrate that dietary sugars also have an effect on blood pressure, caused by the effects of weight gain.

Sugar is thought to have an addictive quality, which has been dramatically confirmed in other mammals. One study repeatedly fed rats an excessive intake of sugar, which induced production of an opioid (naloxone). When the sugar was withdrawn, the rats displayed behavioural signs of opioid withdrawal: chattering teeth, paw tremors and head shakes. Further tests showed that naloxone decreases extracellular dopamine (DA) and increases acetylcholine (ACh), and the DA/ACh imbalance caused withdrawal symptoms that are qualitatively similar to those induced by withdrawal from morphine or nicotine. This suggests that mammals can become sugar dependent, and reducing sugar intake can cause withdrawal symptoms. This only occurs with excessive intake, but a diet high in SSBs and other sweet foods can lead to excessive consumption in humans too.

The massive increase in obesity in the US since the 1980s is correlated with increased caloric intake of about 12 per cent between 1985 and 2000, which itself is largely due to the increased consumption of grains, added fats and added sugars, and the associated increase in carbohydrates. Fruit and SSBs account for a large percentage of this increase. We also have, particularly in the US, the advent of ultra-processed foods. These are products that often have no noticeable standard food product (fruits, wheats, nuts, meats, etc.) mentioned in the labelling. The mainstay in many US convenience stores, ultra-processed food is not intended to provide the basic nutrients, but rather is chemically engineered to stimulate dopamine production in the brain to make the consumer crave more. It is designed to be addictive. Governments ban drugs that give highs because they are addictive, but allow the food-manufacturing industry to create products which are specifically designed to be addictive. These developments in food production are also associated with the growth in a snacking culture, rather than with more formal regular meals. Snacking has been shown to be associated with weight gain (largely because one tends to eat more overall by snacking).

Showing that increased consumption of SSBs and other highly processed and ultra-processed foods is correlated with the massive increase in obesity levels still does not explain why people eat and drink more of these products. The answer is relatively straightforward. We know from simple demand theory that, as food prices fall, consumption will rise. Food prices have fallen relative to other goods over the past 40 years, and the falls have been greatest in calorie-dense, pre-packaged and pre-prepared foods. The relative price of food overall fell on average by around 15 per cent, but the prices of fresh fruits and vegetables rose by 118 per cent, fish by 77 per cent and dairy products by 56 per cent. Thus, the fall in the prices of meat, pre-packaged and pre-prepared foods and soft drinks are even greater relative to less calorie-dense food. People are not only eating more than they were, but are eating more energy-dense fast foods. Even those who are not eating greater quantities than in the past are eating a higher proportion of energy-dense fast foods.

We might also consider the effects of 'food deserts' brought to the attention of people in the US by Michele Obama in 2008. A food desert is an area where residents do not have access to a supermarket. For example, in South Bend, Memphis, the two closest supermarkets are 4.8 miles apart – in an area where one third of households do not have access to a car. If you live somewhere roughly halfway between the two supermarkets you will, if you are healthy, have a brisk 50-minute walk to get the opportunity to buy quality food. If you are old, sick, disabled or indeed obese, you might find that walk problematic. The only places you have to buy your food are fast food restaurants or convenience stores that only sell food products such as high-sugar carbonated drinks, crisps (or chips) and cookies, and other such snacks, including ultra-processed foods. In other words, many people eat low-nutrition, weight-inducing foods because that is all that there is available to them. It is estimated that around 23 million US citizens live in 'food deserts' where there are plenty of food outlets, but ones that only provide the kind of food that, eaten regularly in not particularly large quantities, will make you obese.

What to do?

Governments have reacted to the obesity problem by putting the full burden of responsibility on their citizens. Their response, almost in entirety, has been to persuade people to live more healthily, mounting campaigns advising people to eat more fruit and vegetables, warning of the dangers of excess sugars and salts, and so on. Various countries and some US states now require food labels and restaurants to state the calorific value of foods and give details of what they contain. While this information is useful to the consumer, and there is certainly nothing wrong with providing it, the entire philosophy behind this nudge-style information provision is to place responsibility firmly upon individuals. We know that the middle class, the educated and those with time to read about and understand the effects of different sorts of food additives can make use of the information. The poor, the uneducated and those with little time will not. And some, those in food deserts, cannot. Government information and health drives do nothing to help them.

Governments could easily intervene more directly and effectively using their regulatory powers and the tax system. They could ban the addition of sweeteners, or impose excise or sales taxes on beverages with sweeteners added. They could ban ultra-processed foodstuffs with no nutritional value. Or they could tax beverages that exceed a threshold of grams of added sweetener or kcal per ounce. They could impose taxes assessed per gram of added sugar. All of these simple proposals would promote calorie reduction and encourage manufacturers to reformulate products. Switching from a conventional sweetener-added soft drink of 20 ounces (570 ml) to one below these thresholds would reduce consumption of around 175 fewer calories per drink. This is not an inconsiderable amount, since by some (rough) estimates if you eat 2,000–2,500 calories a day (depending on body size), three such drinks a day will see you gain approximately a pound or half a kilogram per week, every week.

Specific excise taxes are preferable to sales taxes, since the idea is to encourage manufacturers to produce healthier drinks. The taxes would be paid at source by the manufacturers and seen by consumers only at the point of sale – and then only if manufacturers did not respond by changing their products. As the poor are large consumers of such drinks, demand is likely to be quite elastic, so prices would not be affected. Instead, the effects would be on the product itself, and if people liked the adjusted product less, so drank fewer, that would also have health benefits. It has been conservatively estimated that consumers would replace 25 per cent of the calories produced in this way by calories in other forms, leading to an overall 10 per cent reduction in calorie consumption; the benefits would be greater for higher-volume consumers, who are more likely to be overweight or obese.

More controversially, we might also want to tax beverages containing non-caloric sweeteners. While these do not directly lead to weight problems (though they may be associated with other health risks: recently some non-caloric sweeteners have been implicated in increased risks of cancer), there is evidence that they habituate the palate to extreme sweetness and so encourage the consumption of other high-calorie foodstuffs.

Judging the evidence

Obesity is a more complex issue than gun control. Very few people actually deny the evidence that lax gun laws increase mortality and injury rates. To be sure, politicians and gun lobbyists try to deflect attention away from gun regulations by pointing to personal responsibility and to the psychology of shooters, or they argue that if everyone were armed, victims could shoot back (though they offer no evidence that this would actually lower the death rate). In the main, however, there is no serious attempt to dispute the facts. The academic task is to establish whether trends in the death and injury rates can be ascribed to particular changes in regulations.

The so-called obesity crisis is different: here the scientific evidence is challenged. The challenges are directed not at the evidence itself – the fact that obesity is increasing – but at the idea that obesity is a problem at all, or at views of its underlying causes, particularly the level of personal responsibility involved. Readers can judge for themselves, from the figures I have outlined, whether or not obesity is a problem. The fundamental argument of this book is that, while people do bear some personal responsibility, the incidence and distribution of body-shape and obesity problems are to be laid at the door of government. We ought, nevertheless, to seriously consider the idea that the problem has multiple causes, and not simply blame the substances added in modern food manufacture.

The scientific evidence on the relationship between sugars, fats and carbohydrates and their effects on body shape is mixed, and different studies do not all agree. As I described in the opening chapter, one response to mixed evidence is to throw doubt upon the very fact that we have any scientific evidence at all. However, that is not true and, as I explained there, we can learn a lot from systematic review and meta-analysis, from which much of my evidence given in this chapter is taken.

Still, people sometimes claim that, despite this evidence, science does not 'really know' what causes the increase in obesity around the world and therefore we can have no confidence in any regulatory processes. This response is daft. Does anyone actually think that there is one, and only one, cause of increasing obesity? Sugars, sweeteners, saturated fats, and so on, can all have an effect independently of each other or in concert. We have evidence that they all have effects on the growing rates of obesity, but the evidence on which is the main cause is mixed. To say that, since we don't know the precise details of how each of the different components in manufactured food affects health, therefore we should do nothing is not a rational response. Better to respond that, if it has been shown that they all have an effect, then perhaps we should regulate them all.

Let us say, for some reason – time constraints, perhaps – that regulating them all is not possible. Do we therefore conclude that we should do nothing? Clearly, we should regulate one of them, the one against which, on balance, the evidence is strongest, or one simply chosen at random. Doing nothing because one is not sure which course of action would be best is to act in the manner of Jean Buridan's famous donkey, who starved to death because he could not decide which bundle of hay was the nicer. Governments and societies should not be so asinine.

We may also note that the amount of food we eat, or the proportion of sugars in it, might not have such a pronounced effect on health if we did not live such sedentary lifestyles. However, regulating lifestyles by, for example, making cycling to work compulsory or mandating attendance at fitness camps, is much more difficult to enforce; and here, surely, libertarian arguments have strong traction. So, while it is true that regulating food manufacture more tightly might not fully deal with the issue, because other lifestyle factors also have an effect, this does not mean that regulation will not have some effect. We can still use nudge processes to encourage healthier lifestyles (and indeed healthy eating); regulating and nudging are not incompatible. However, nudging is less effective in many areas than regulating, and it should be used alongside regulations, not in place of them. (I discuss the nudge alternative in Chapter 7.)

Third, policy analysts, particularly those influenced by discourse analysis and critical theory, often suggest that there are different discourses and communities of belief. This 'rival narrative approach' leads writers to take the obvious evidence that different sets of people have different views, and tend to use different types of phrases and rhetorical devices to push their viewpoints, to reach the conclusion that *therefore* each approach is equally valid and we cannot make any definitive judgement. Each community, it is asserted, has its own interests, and it is these that drive the conclusion, not the evidence and argument deployed by that community. In this way, scientific evidence on the effects of additives in food manufacture is downgraded to the level of any old claim.

There are two strong reasons why the inference from the obvious premise to the conclusion (marked by my italicized *therefore*) is fallacious. First, while there is no doubt that scientists, like everyone else, have biases and self-interests, the scientific method is designed to mitigate those interests. The main self-interest of scientists is getting their research published and cited. Careers are made by publishing, and publishing in the top scientific journals and having others recognize your work by citing it in their own work is how scientists progress their careers. This does indeed tend to create a 'positive publication bias' – that is, results that show a relationship between variables are more likely to be published than ones that do not. This also gives incentives for scientists to look for positive evidence, for evidence that shows a relationship between some independent variable (for example, sugar) and some dependent variable (such as weight gain).

However, this publication bias is well known in science. The review processes of the major journals, and new practices adopted over the last decade or so, try to overcome it. Furthermore, the scientific process involves replication. Many studies attempt to replicate previous studies, and here, failing to confirm the previous results is likely to lead to publication and citation. Hence the scientific method itself is designed to overcome positive publication bias.

The area that we need to be more sceptical about is when research conducted into food and health is funded and carried out under the auspices of food manufacturers. They have an even more direct interest in trying to downgrade any evidence linking their products to ill health. Science journals now insist that researchers specify who paid for the research and any pecuniary or other interest they have that might impugn their research findings. So that source of bias is also mitigated, to some extent, at least in the major and reputable scientific journals.

Furthermore, placing greater evidential weight on systematic review and meta-analysis also helps us to overcome the bias that might exist in individual studies. In this regard, it should be noted that my arguments in this book do not rely upon the claim that 'so-and-so' has just found this important effect, therefore government should immediately do such-and-such. It is just that sort of knee-jerk reaction of governments to immediate policy problems picked up by the media that leads to bad policy. Everything I claim we know, and government should act upon, is based on studies over many years, replicated and systematically reviewed. The evidence is strong.

The final aspect of the 'rival narrative' approach to thinking about the issue of obesity of which we should be suspicious is that the narratives are not actually rivals. To be sure, some emphasize individual responsibility for health, and some emphasize the structured opportunities, that is, the regulatory system within which individuals make their choices. Once we understand that we can only judge how responsible people are in comparison with others in similar choice situations, then we can recognize the extent to which people are responsible for their own health. If you and I have similar backgrounds, upbringing, education, social class and so forth, and one of us is obese and the other not, then we can make the judgement that, relative to each other, we are responsible for our different body sizes. Of course, we might challenge even that claim, if we can point to specific differences, in genes perhaps, or in our incentive structures. There might be a particular incident which happened to you and not to me; had it occurred the other way round, to me and not to you, our lifestyles would also have been turned around. That is a favourite science fiction narrative. We cannot really make these judgements, only offer plausible stories.

However, when we aggregate many cases, across types of people, the specific incidents that cause differences within types are washed out. That is the value of statistical analyses across type. Here we are not making any judgements about personal responsibility. We are only looking at the structures that create different incentives across type. We can confidently say that the poor gain weight because, for them, the incentive to buy cheap unhealthy food is greater than for the middle class and rich. To deny that claim is to deny any such claim about incentives. Those right-wing commentators who place the entire burden on personal responsibility seem to deny the relevance of such incentive structures, yet it is precisely the same mechanism that leads us to believe that price increases reduce demand, that making it harder for people to enter a country will reduce immigration and that tougher sentences will deter crime. They accept the role of incentive structures in these cases, but not in obesity.

There is a second and important aspect of the fact that rival narratives are not actually rivals: the conclusions to be drawn from them are not rivals. Some of the narratives suggest that health problems in society are caused by social dislocation. That might be the case. That does not mean that the medical evidence is wrong, nor that regulation might not help reduce the problems. It might be that there is moral panic over the obesity issue, leading to inflated rhetoric, but that does not mean the medical evidence is impugned, nor that regulation will not help reduce the problem. And, alongside changing diets through regulation (by making it impossible or expensive to eat food with such high sugar and salt content), we can also use nudge tactics to get people to choose healthier food from the choices available and to exercise more.

The final aspect is that to recognize medical experts is not to dismiss other expertise, including personal experience. The extent of the obesity problem has been shown by several sets of experts. Epidemiologists have statistically demonstrated it in populations. Medical researchers have identified, both experimentally with non-human mammals and statistically across types of people, the effects of specific additives in food manufacture. Other experimental and theoretical researchers are beginning to tease out the bodily causal mechanisms that lead sugars and fats to cause weight problems, and indeed to understand why, genetically, some people have a greater propensity to obesity than others. There are many other sorts of experts, too: those, for instance, who specialize in what types of exercise help people in what circumstances. There is also the experience of ordinary people, especially those who experience weight problems.

A movement against fat shaming is growing. The idea is that people deemed to be overweight are not necessarily unhappy, and any unhappiness they have with their weight is caused by others pointing out that they are fat or obese. Obese people are made to feel ashamed of their bodies because of the weight of public opinion.

My argument is that we should not place the burden of responsibility for body shape on to people personally, but to recognize that government, and the society that elects governments to regulate as they will, are responsible. This argument should relieve and not add to the fat-shaming problem: both directly, because people will no longer be blamed for their weight problems, and, more importantly, indirectly, because government resources and efforts will switch from nudging people – framing issues to lead people to be aware of body shape and what they can do to achieve the body form experts think is healthiest – to creating incentives for them to become healthier without even trying. Regulation at source will ease the problems associated with fat shaming because it recognizes that, while people are responsible for the choices they make given the opportunities they have available, regulating what goes into manufactured foods will give them better opportunities to live the lifestyle they want without so many of the potential downsides.

No individual responsibility?

I have repeatedly claimed that the increase in body-shape problems in society is the responsibility of government. That is not to say that individuals bear no responsibility for their own body shape. However, the extent to which people are responsible for their actions is relative to the incentives they face. If two people face similar incentives to behave one way or another, then the extent to which they are responsible, relative to each other, can be measured by the different choices they make. People are never identical. Even identical twins have different experiences in life, and there are no genetic factors that cause people both to have stronger preferences for sweet or fatty foods and to experience different metabolic reactions to eating those foods. When considering individual responsibility, these facts are important. However, the increase in obesity since the 1980s cannot be put down to genetics, since there are no genetic changes in humankind that could have had that kind of effect. Could there be any other factors that impinge on personal responsibility?

Some right-wing newspaper columnists seem to think that the rise in obesity is due to some major psychological change in the population and that, indeed, the government is to blame for this state of affairs. The 'nanny state', they assert, is responsible for the obesity epidemic. They claim that government intervention has disrupted the social equilibrium of personal responsibility, leading people to expect the state to step in, rather than taking care of themselves. It is hard to reconstruct what the causal mechanism for these claims is supposed to be. But it seems to be the idea that, because of welfare payments, poor people are able to afford to buy junk food, and have cars, and are then provided with a health service that keeps them going when they get fat. In the good old days, the poor survived on potatoes and thin soups, walked or cycled everywhere, and knew that if they had health problems they would die, so they took better care of themselves.

I suppose that offering free surgery for the morbidly obese could be an example of 'disruptive' government intervention, but generally such pundits supply no evidence to back up their claims. Indeed, given that, since the end of the 1970s, the welfare state has been significantly cut back in Australia, the UK and the US, and neoliberal market capitalism given freer rein and encouragement, it would seem that giving greater responsibility to individuals or, at least, governments abnegating any responsibility is the more obvious causal mechanism.

Of course, our society would be different if fewer people drove cars. And we could return to the mortality and morbidity rates of the 1930s if we really wanted that as a public policy initiative. When it comes to food, however, the problem is precisely the opposite: junk and manufactured food is cheap, and getting hold of good-quality fresh food is often beyond the means of the poor, who do not have the resources (money, time, transport) to obtain it readily. Regulating might actually increase personal responsibility, rather than decreasing it, by levelling out the costs of fresh and highly processed food. In any case, it is not the job of government to regulate personal responsibility. It is the job of government to take responsibility for the level and distribution of welfare in the society it governs given the distribution of responsible behaviour in society. There is actually no evidence that people, even teenagers, are less responsible than they used to be. The old always hold that opinion, but no one has ever attempted to demonstrate that it is true.

What is interesting in the debate on obesity is that the nanny state argument, at least in Australia and the UK, is pressed by only a tiny minority of shock commentators in relatively few media outlets. Their views are given wider currency by a few politicians, but among the broader debate of health experts, policy experts and the wider public debate, the nanny state is simply not an issue. Most people want their governments to come up with policies that look after their welfare, while they get on with living their lives as best as they can. It is somewhat ironic that so many liberal and left-wing political theorists worry about 'state paternalism' when, at least in the major public arenas, only the most marginal right-wing commentators, and those powerful enough to dominate and exploit others, give a damn about it.

Final word

Obesity is an emotive topic. People are right to demand an end to fat shaming. Nevertheless, obesity is a health problem about which we should be concerned. The fast-rising rates of obesity have occurred following the transformation of food manufacture from the 1960s onwards, compounded by modern lifestyles where we exercise less, both in our workplace and in our leisure time. If governments were to act on the first element, then they would not need to declaim so vociferously on the second. It is right for health experts to point out what foods are good for us, but not to blame citizens who cannot afford them or even gain access to them. Fat shaming should end, with government taking full responsibility for the rising rates of obesity by recognizing its regulatory failures and ensuring that food manufacturers reduce the number of fat-inducing additives in their products. The alternative might be legal class action against food manufacturers to induce them to change their products.

4

Homelessness

Homelessness as a major problem in the developed world re-emerged in the 1980s. What was the cause of its reappearance? Politicians are keen to blame citizens. Australian Treasurer Joe Hockey in 2015 advised young people wanting to buy their first home to 'get a good job that pays good money', while property developer Tim Gurner suggested that young Australians could not afford to buy his developments because they waste money on fancy toast and overpriced coffee. Australian Prime Minister Malcolm Turnbull had another solution in 2016: he suggested that their wealthy parents should buy homes for them.

If indeed the growing homelessness in Australia and other countries is really due to individual or household irresponsibility, then we have to explain why people became more irresponsible at that time. The alternative explanation is that, around the world, governments changed their housing policies. And, by and large, they did. First, they created a massive bias in the tax system that rewarded not only home owners, but also rentiers. Second, governments stopped seeing their role as providing affordable public housing for the poor, both directly and through keeping down private rents through rent control. Governments began to see political advantages in opening up private home ownership, both through the tax system and by selling off public housing on the cheap.

In the UK, for example, there were large stocks of public housing, provided and maintained by local councils. In the 1980s the Thatcher government brought in the 'right-to-buy' policy for council tenants. Much of that existing housing stock was sold below market price. At the same time, the government restricted local councils' capacity to build new public housing, tying up the reserves they had for building. They began to provide incentives for councils to stop directly managing public housing, encouraging the growth of housing trusts, and thereby removing local government from its role in housing provision. Similarly, in both Australia and the US, the social provision of housing has been reduced over time despite growing needs. In the US, $3 billion was cut from Housing and Urban Development between 2010 and 2018 (around 7 per cent of its budget). In Australia, the number of public housing builds reduced from an average 15,500 per annum in the 1950s to the 1970s to averaging only 6,000 per annum since then. These figures also hide the precipitous drop from 12,000 a year in the mid-1970s to around 4,000 today.

At the same time that government was getting out of the business of directly providing social housing, its environmental policies (such as green-field laws), requirements on infrastructure and other planning changes made it more difficult for private developers to build low-cost housing. This is another aspect of government getting out of the housing business, since requirements pertaining to infrastructure, for example, are attempts to transfer more costs to developers and away from local government.

In 2015–16, the charity Homelessness Australia received 279,000 applications for assistance – an increase of 14 per cent from 244,000 in 2012–13 – and were unable to help in 70,653 cases. Homelessness Australia estimates that the country has a shortfall of over 500,000 affordable rental dwellings that are available to households on the lowest 40 per cent of incomes. In June 2016, there were 194,592 applicants waiting for social housing, of whom around 59,000 people were considered to be in great need.

We see similar relative numbers in the US. There it is estimated that there are around 550,000 homeless people, of whom about a third are rough sleepers, and about 35 per cent are families with children. The manifest observation is of rough sleepers, and the scarcity of public facilities increases the public nuisance aspect. Few public authorities now provide free public bathroom and toilet facilities; rough sleepers cannot attempt to keep clean and so they soil parks and roadways. Alcohol and drug problems are rife among rough sleepers and there is a growing problem of dirty hypodermic needles discarded in roads and parks. With few institutional facilities or publicly funded help for the mentally ill, there are also increasing numbers of people on the street with severe psychological and mental problems. (Another policy area I could have studied, where recent government policy in the developed world has exacerbated problems, is mental health.)

Private landowners sometimes attempt to move rough sleepers away from their property by installing metal bumps on the pavement or in doorway shelters to make it more uncomfortable to sleep, or by – illegally – erecting fences in public areas. Some cities attempt to literally displace rough sleepers by providing bus tickets to other places, ostensibly to locations where the homeless were born or arrived from. Rough sleeping affects not only welfare, but also freedom. With no public bathroom facilities and increasing efforts to stop rough sleepers using toilets in shops, cafes and bars, and policing of water features in towns, the homeless lose the freedom to carry out the most basic human needs. Policy has been short-termist, lacking any vision for dealing with the problems, with no aim other than shifting the worst aspects of homelessness away from the sight of those who have homes. But growing gentrification has both revealed and exacerbated the problems, as the better off move back into central city areas, making affordable housing where job opportunities reside more problematic. People can afford to live where they cannot find work, but cannot afford to live where they can find work. Cities with effective urban transport systems can cope with this problem, but many metropolitan communities have experienced the breakdown of public transport. As we shall see below, however, the major problem in the US is the changes to the regulatory framework for meeting housing needs that started in the 1970s.

At the same time as governments were slowly getting out of the business of providing housing, they encouraged the private market for housing. Removing rent controls pushes up the price of dwellings as investment properties, while various tax advantages encourage home ownership. The justification for removing rent control is to encourage new builds, but any new builds that are thereby encouraged do not make up for the vanished state investment in housing. Furthermore, new builds and rentable properties are directed at different markets. Developers want to build properties that go for higher rents, and those who buy to let prefer to rent to higher-income earners. So affordable housing is left behind. Or, when low rents are offered, the buildings are of poor quality, with tenants packed in, so the profit margins remain high.

Other tax policies (discussed below) even encourage landlords to leave properties empty rather than attract tenants with lower rents. This has happened to such an extent that rates of home ownership from about the mid-1990s began to fall for the first time (apart from a dip in the 1930s depression in the US) since the end of the 19th century, as owning becomes unaffordable for larger numbers of people. Median house prices have risen to over seven times median incomes in large cities in the US, UK and Australia, where three times median income has usually been seen as the 'affordable' rate. Of course, rent control also encourages those who might otherwise buy to rent, and we can regulate rents to the extent we can encourage new builds. There are different ways to operate rent control: a regulatory agency setting fair rents, for example, is far superior to freezing rents – one of the more ridiculous ways to implement rent control policy.

These are just facts about how markets operate. The growing problem of homelessness is a direct result of government policies that have developed over the past 40 years. We cannot blame those who are homeless for the lack of affordable housing, nor point to private renters and developers who are responding to the incentives that governments have given them. We shall see that almost every government policy in the US, UK and Australia over the past 40 years or so has compounded the housing crisis. We will examine those government policies in a little more detail after we have looked at the growing problems of homelessness in the developed world.

What is homelessness?

When we think of homelessness, we tend to think of people living rough in the street. However, such 'rough sleepers' are only a fraction of those households, individuals and families that are actually homeless. In British law, indeed, virtually no rough sleeper is deemed to be legally homeless. The definition of homelessness under British law denotes the statutory right of someone to be housed by local authorities. The 1977 Housing (Homeless Persons) Act, reinforced by Part III of the 1985 Housing Act, obliges a local authority to accept an application for housing only if the applicant (1) is homeless or under threat of homelessness within 28 days, (2) is in 'priority need', (3) is not 'intentionally' homeless and (4) is able to show a local connection. The claim that one's accommodation is unsatisfactory does not make one homeless. A young person leaving home because of abuse or bad parental relations might be deemed to have made themselves intentionally homeless, as may a person who leaves after threats of violence. The key element of the Act is 'priority need', which in practice covers only families with children, pregnant women, the elderly, mentally ill, disabled and 'disaster victims'. So, by law, few lone adults, even if sleeping in the street, are statutorily homeless. In the UK, the average age of a rough sleeper when they die is 43 – about half the average life expectancy. The number of rough sleepers has doubled over the past decade.

Academics understand homelessness as a multifaceted concept. It can be taken to mean literally 'no accommodation', but scholars more generally define it as meaning no secure or adequate accommodation, as in the Australian Bureau of Statistics (ABS) definition:

> if they do not have suitable accommodation alternatives and their current living arrangement:
> - is in a dwelling that is inadequate;
> - has no tenure, or if their initial tenure is short and not extendable; or
> - does not allow them to have control of, and access to space for social relations.

The ABS estimates that the rate of homelessness in Australia has increased by 4.6 per cent from 2011 to 2016. On census night 2016, 116,000 people were experiencing homelessness (that is 5 per 1,000 people, or 0.5 per cent of the population). The ABS estimates that a quarter of homeless people are aged between 20 and 30, though the numbers aged 65 to 74 also increased between 2011 and 2016. Recent migrants (arrived in the five years prior to the 2016 census) account for 15 per cent. Aboriginal and Torres Strait Islander people made up around 20 per cent of those experiencing homelessness in 2016.

Other definitions of homelessness in Australia include the 'Chamberlain and Mackenzie' definition that breaks homelessness down into three categories: primary, where a person is without conventional accommodation, including sleeping rough in the streets, cars or abandoned buildings; secondary, where someone resides in temporary accommodation, moving regularly; and tertiary, where someone lives in a boarding or non-self-contained dwelling with no security of tenure. This definition is utilized in Australian primary legislation on homelessness.

Personal responsibility for homelessness

There is no question that certain types of people are more likely to become homeless than others. Rough sleepers are seven times more likely to be dependent upon drugs or alcohol, and around two thirds of those blame their drug or alcohol addiction for their homeless state. If those dependent on drugs were provided with secure accommodation, they would not be homeless, and they might no longer be dependent upon drugs or alcohol. The strong correlation between being homeless and such addictions would also be shown to be what it is. Long term, the causal link is largely the other way around: drug dependency increases the longer one has been homeless. Being homeless, along with being in jail, is the most extreme form of social exclusion, and it is hardly surprising that the socially excluded, cold and hungry, find solace and removal from the harsh reality of their daily life through drink and drugs. Certainly, it is harder to quit drug or alcohol dependence if one is homeless than if one has secure accommodation, so there is also a causal link from homelessness to drug and alcohol dependence.

It is also clear that people with cognitive disabilities and mental health problems are more likely to end up homeless than those without such disabilities or psychological problems. Researchers find that some rough sleepers do make the choice to spend resources on drugs rather than shelter, and that some rough sleepers choose to leave secure accommodation because of family or relationship problems there. Some studies suggest that rough sleeping can be a cultural choice made by, for example, Indigenous Australians. One should be rightly sceptical of these studies, which are highly theoretical, not usually made by those who study specific cultures and provide scant empirical evidence other than what a selected few rough sleepers say. People are wont to justify themselves, especially when they do not feel in control. Besides, even if these findings suggest that sleeping rough might be a lifestyle choice for a few, that should not affect our attitudes to the many.

In other words, we can explain, to some extent, why some individuals end up homeless while others do not, and we can apportion some relative responsibility to people for being in the homeless category. However, while 'care in the community' has tended to leave more mentally ill people homeless and drug addiction has increased, neither of these effects are great enough to explain the increase in rough sleeping. Furthermore, as we shall see, giving people homes is one of the best ways of helping them overcome mental illness and drug addiction. The causal process operates in both directions. The idea that more people are choosing to sleep rough than in the past is ridiculous, so we cannot use personal responsibility to explain the rise in homelessness over the past 40 years or so. Also, we must acknowledge the great rise in homelessness outside of rough sleeping includes large numbers of people who are working. So we cannot look to personal responsibility; we have to look at structural changes in society. Choices made by the state, the government and society, are what explains the growing homelessness problem, not choices made by individuals themselves.

More poor people are living in non-permanent accommodation because states are providing fewer low-cost homes and failing to ensure that rentable properties are affordable and available. Governments have encouraged the property boom that makes many people better off through investment income at the expense of those who cannot afford to invest. And these policies have been deliberate and wilful. Responsibility for the amount and distribution of homelessness in modern society sits squarely with those who govern, and not with the homeless themselves.

Government policies on homelessness

US

The history of housing policy from the late 1960s until today is a catalogue of changes that have created a homelessness crisis and forged the global economic crisis of 2008. The Housing Act of 1937 required that public housing units be clearly obsolescent before they could be demolished or converted to other usages. A 1969 amendment required that any housing unit that was abolished had to be replaced by a unit of similar size and function. In 1985, this one-for-one replacement programme was abandoned. Between 1985 and 2012, over 260,000 public housing units were demolished with no replacement put in place.

This came about, in part, because of ideas that took hold in the late 20th century, which suggested that concentrating public housing in large estates or projects lumped the urban poor together, contributing to a deteriorating environment, which fostered depressed attitudes, bad behaviour, growing drug problems and crime. But these estates also became run down, in part, because public housing authorities (PHAs) allowed this to happen.

While the one-for-one replacement programme was abolished in 1985, PHAs could still only demolish public housing if it was clearly obsolescent. In 1992, the National Commission on Severely Distressed Public Housing (NCSDPH) issued a report that, as the HOPE VI initiative, developed into a programme of large-scale demolition. The NCSDPH allowed estates to be demolished if families there were in distress (measured by school drop-out rates, unemployment and median income); there were high rates of crime; there were management problems (high vacancy rates, low rates of rent collection); or the physical condition of the buildings was poor. This was a recipe for PHAs to not invest in their estates. By not investing in their housing stock, they allowed estates to become wastelands that could then be redeveloped. As development occurred in major cities, public housing became 'islands of decay in seas of renewal'. Private developers were keen to acquire them as the middle class started to return to the inner cities; huge profits awaited if prime real estate could be bought and developed into high-priced townhouses and apartments. PHAs were willing accomplices, given the fiscal gains for local governments alongside big profits for private developers. Analysis demonstrates that cities with the greatest upward movement in land prices were also those that demolished the most public housing during the 1990s.

While NCSDPH reaffirmed the importance of public housing, and wanted to preserve it – the report considered only 6 per cent was severely distressed – it created the incentive for PHAs to get rid of vast amounts of public housing. Many urban liberals supported the break-up of the public housing estates in the hope that mixed development would encourage better standards of living for the urban poor. The belief that more private renting would also encourage geographical and hence labour mobility also saw a shift away from direct public provision of housing. So changing ideas about housing policy fitted well with the large-scale demolition of public housing. Of course, the problem was that the mixed-housing provision and the private rental market did not even begin to adequately cover the loss of public housing.

US housing policy had shifted from trying to solve the housing problems of the poor to an ambitious plan to revitalize urban communities. However, this entailed changing them into communities of the newly migrated middle class and professionals – the gentrification of urban areas – not the improvement of the lot of those who already lived there. HOPE VI normalized demolition and dismantled the public housing stock. The very idea of the 1930s New Deal, that any demolition of public housing could only occur if it was obsolete, and the 1960s idea of one-for-one replacement, was long gone.

I do not wish to exaggerate the good effects of the New Deal on homelessness. Much public housing was not subsidized and much of it went to providing rental housing for the white middle classes, though increasing housing stock did affect private rental prices. And the policy for dwellings built under the New

Deal as part of the Public Works Administration was explicitly racist, in that new housing had to be made available through a 'neighbourhood composition rule' that meant housing in white areas was only for whites, in black areas only for blacks. And most housing was provided in white areas. Nonetheless, the project did fund affordable housing.

Relaxing banking regulations also encouraged private borrowing and home ownership. The 1980s Savings and Loans crisis saw the failure of almost a third (1,403 out of 3,234) saving and loan associations in the US, as interest rates were put up to curb inflation when they had lent money at fixed rates. They were allowed to take out risky investments in order to try to cover losses, which just compounded their problems. The deregulation of the savings and loan industry by two congressional laws, the Depository Institutions Deregulation and Monetary Control Act (1980) and the Garn–St. Germain Depository Institutions Act of 1982, were primary causes of these problems.

The global financial crisis of 2007–8 was similarly a result of deregulation and laxer financial rules. It occurred as credit problems transpired when sub-prime mortgage holders reneged on lending, causing a crisis of confidence in investors in the value of these debts, resulting in a liquidity crisis. We can see this as, at base, a problem of those who could not afford to buy being persuaded to do so – by ideology, by offers of unrealistic loans – causing house prices to rise to unsustainable levels. The problem lies not only in lax regulation, but also in the ideology of home ownership, and the fact that in a high-home-ownership society it is irrational not to want to buy. Indeed, increasingly provision for the elderly is presuming they own their own homes. The problem is also caused by the lack of affordable rentable accommodation. Governments abandoning the business of directly providing affordable housing, lifting rent controls and relaxing lending regulations cause these problems.

UK

After the Second World War, the UK government implemented an integrated strategy of building new houses. War damage had to be rectified, and investment in homes was seen as a priority.

Government intervened in various ways, relaxing planning regulations, enabling some compulsory purchase orders, and so on. Over the next 30 years, cities saw the demolition of substandard and obsolete buildings and major new public building schemes, both houses and high-rise flats, while new towns were built on former farmland and other green-field sites.

The efforts were coordinated through central and local government, with the latter largely in charge of both planning regulations and public or council housing. Most of the costs of the building programme were met through central government taxation. In this way, a large council house stock was built up by the late 1970s. Councils were also responsible for rent control: tenants could appeal against high rents, and a system was in place to assess a reasonable rent for the type and condition of the property. There were problems, of course: some council housing estates were run down and crime-ridden, and the high-rise 'brutalist block' dwellings built in the 1950s and 1960s were soon seen as failures and unsuitable accommodation for families. Arguments also abounded that rent control did not encourage people to rent out rooms or buildings, squeezing the private market out of provision. Nor had homelessness been eradicated, and there were still large-scale rentiers exploiting the poor with substandard accommodation. Nevertheless, the problems were to get much worse.

The post-war consensus, in which government was seen as the major provider of dwellings and the chief regulator of the private rental market, began to break down with the election of a Conservative government under Margaret Thatcher in 1979. Conservative ideology pursued taking power away from local government and giving it to the people. The incoming government began with the Priority Estates Project, designed to save run-down estates. It was a direct intervention by central government into council-run estates, bringing in new local management to estates in appalling condition. The direct involvement of tenants was a feature of the scheme, which was quickly regarded as a success.

In 1980 the government introduced the 'right-to-buy' programme, giving council tenants the right to purchase their residence from the council. In 1981 it created Development

Corporations, again taking control away from local councils, in an attempt to redevelop around 1.1 million unfit houses (some damaged in a series of major inner-city riots). In 1985, Estate Action once more targeted run-down estates, shifting responsibility for housing from elected local councils to estate management boards. The sale of council housing helped fire up prices, as did the relaxation of lending rules (furthermore, banks started lending practices that were later deemed illegal). Steep increases in interest rates caused problems for those with mortgages and discouraged new buyers. House prices having risen from 1979, the housing market collapsed in the late 1980s. While it was largely the better off who bought their homes, the housing market meant that some former council tenants lost the houses they had purchased, but by British law were not deemed homeless.

The 1988 Housing Act introduced assured tenancies, promoted the transfer of housing stock away from council control and introduced Housing Action Trusts (HATs). Any council estate could set up its own HAT outside council control, while some housing departments within councils were turned into HATs. 'Tenants' Choice' enabled these processes even against the objections of the local council involved. From this point onwards, HATs became the major developers of social housing, using private finance. In 1991, City Challenge was launched: another initiative to establish quasi-business public–private partnerships for inner-city areas in decline. By 1992, councils were increasingly forced by compulsory competitive tendering to shift more of their housing stock to HATs. The 1996 Housing Act created registered social landlords and local housing companies and further restricted homeless people's rights to council housing.

The incoming Labour government of 1997 did not change direction when it came to housing policy. It created the Social Exclusion Unit to examine the worst housing problems, but its first major legislation was the 2002 Homeless Act, intended to encourage development of local strategies to help prevent homelessness and deliver partnerships between the public and private sectors. Recognizing the relationship between housing problems and health, the 2003 Housing Bill sought to reintegrate housing and health issues more closely, but coordination between housing and health authorities remains problematic. One of the problems has been that housing authorities and health authorities have different budgets geared towards different purposes, so they shift responsibilities.

The coalition and Conservative governments of the 21st century have extended the right-to-buy programme beyond council houses to HATs (though not to private landlords). The 2016 Housing and Planning Act also forced councils to sell off high-value stock and prioritize the (private) building of 'starter homes' to further encourage home ownership.

All of these policies over the past 40 years have been aimed at getting government out of the business of directly providing dwellings and at encouraging private renting and home ownership. They have had the effect of inflating house prices: since the collapse in the mid-1980s, house price growth in the UK has averaged 2.4 per cent per annum compared to a European average of 1.1 per cent, and between 1995 and 2014 averaged 2.7 per cent. Affordability has dropped dramatically, with around 30 per cent of new households able to buy in the 2010s, compared to 45 per cent in the mid-1980s.

With devolution, Scotland embarked on a slightly different route from the rest of the UK on housing policy, as elsewhere. With regard to rights, Scotland has some of the most advanced homelessness legislation anywhere in the world. The Homelessness etc. (Scotland) Act 2003 (Scot) asp 10 provides an enforceable right to settled accommodation for those who are unintentionally homeless. This entitlement extends not only to those in accommodation that is not reasonable to continue to occupy, but to those who have no security, due to threats of violence or overcrowding. Local authorities have an obligation to find accommodation, so negative decisions can be successfully challenged in the courts. Meanwhile, in the last decade, Scotland has built an average of 7,650 affordable homes per year. Since 2003, the number of households seeking accommodation has gone down year on year (until 2018, when there was a 1 per cent rise).

Australia

There are some similarities between the Australian and the British cases, but many differences. The first important difference is that Australia is a federation and the states have constitutional responsibility for housing. The federal (or Commonwealth) government was little involved in housing policy until after the Second World War; it provided some dwellings for returning soldiers at the end of the First World War, built some houses in the new capital of Canberra and set up the Commonwealth Savings Bank to lend money to prospective home owners.

There is great variation in housing policy across the different states. For example, in South Australia, the South Australian Housing Trust (SAHT) was set up in 1936 and was both an urban planner and low-cost-housing provider. After 1945, it became a major developer and public housing authority. The SAHT was created in part to encourage the migration of industry and working people to South Australia, which tended to attract fewer immigrants than its rivals, New South Wales (NSW) and Victoria. The 20th century saw large interstate variation in expenditure per head of population: NSW was the lowest, with South Australia almost three times higher. Housing expenditure mirrors the desire of the states for immigration, with more help offered in states more anxious to attract people. NSW, Victoria and Queensland were the fastest-growing states, and the ones with the least need to attract immigrants. Despite being the first state to provide public housing in 1910, Queensland's policy has been to help people buy houses, and it resisted the efforts of the Commonwealth government to encourage public housing. By the 21st century, Queensland only had 3.5 per cent public housing – half the average of Australia as a whole.

The Commonwealth government started planning for housing during the Second World War as it recognized massive housing problems, both in lack of dwellings and in poor-quality stock. Australia had always had a tradition of people building their own homes, with higher home ownership at the end of the 19th century than in the UK or the US, or indeed around the world generally. While there was little war damage in Australia, the wartime Commonwealth government wanted to provide homes for returning soldiers. It set up the Commonwealth–State

Housing Agreement in 1945, which encouraged states to provide housing, and under its auspices 670,000 houses were built over the next decade, half privately. The agreement was rewritten approximately every five years (until 2009, by then called the National Australian Assistance Plan). By its third iteration, there was a shift away from public build-for-rent as the states moved to preferring home ownership, though in the 1970s and 1980s the Whitlam and the Hawke governments tried to encourage public rental stock.

Over time, these changing agreements have led to a substantial reduction of social housing in real terms, given the growing needs of a population that has been rapidly expanding since the 1990s. Legislation ensures the federal government and the states or territories jointly fund housing initiatives, and sets broad goals to target assistance to those most in need. While the Commonwealth Housing Assistance Act (1996) acknowledges that shelter and housing are a basic need for humans, neither it nor its predecessors (such as the Supported Accommodation Act (1994)) created any rights to accommodation or duties to house people.

The 2007 Rudd government declared that a national affordable homes strategy was a priority, establishing the National Affordable Housing Agreement (2009) and National Partnership Agreements on Homelessness. Yet it aimed to achieve this not through any primary legislation, but simply through the Federal Financial Relations Act (2009) that provides financial support for state programmes, which is its only constitutional path. In 2013, the Labor government introduced the Homelessness Bill, which included provisions recognizing structural (that is, involuntary) causes of homelessness and emphasized obligations that Australia has under international human rights laws, but it did not establish a right to housing or a duty to accommodate those in need. Moreover, Labor's general election defeat that year meant the Bill was never enacted.

Assistance for first-home buyers has been introduced, abolished and re-established numerous times by Commonwealth, state and territory governments since it was first introduced in 1964. Since then, around AUD$24 billion has been spent on first-home buyer grants, pushing house prices upwards. (And, we should note, first-home buyers are not necessarily young people, but include wealthy immigrants.) Despite this expenditure, home ownership has remained at approximately 70 per cent since the early 1960s.

Negative gearing is a Commonwealth policy allowing property losses to be set against other types of income, allowing people to reduce and defer personal tax liabilities. The 1999 Howard government decision to exempt from tax half of capital gains in housing encouraged the buying of second homes and buy-to-let properties. The apparently relentless upward trajectory of house prices also encourages buying property, even if high rental rates mean it stays empty, since losses can be set against other tax liabilities, and the property will still be a valuable investment. Over 15 per cent of Australia's individual taxpayers are now landlords, collectively losing the Commonwealth nearly AUD$8 billion in tax write-offs. Since 92 per cent of such investors buy existing properties, they do little to increase the supply of affordable housing, but contribute instead to the almost one million unoccupied dwellings in the major cities – equivalent to 11 per cent of housing stock. The fact of the matter is that there is more than enough housing for all Australians currently living in the country, and more than enough even in the areas where most of the homeless dwell.

Economic policies such as negative gearing have led to substantial rises in house prices over the past 20 years or so, outpacing income growth and helping to add to the substantial increase in household debt from 140 per cent of national disposable income in 2000 to around 206 per cent by 2014. The largest increases are in the major cities of Sydney and Melbourne, but significant rises have occurred all over Australia. As in the UK and the US, house prices relative to annual income have moved from a ratio of about 2.5 to over 5. While about two thirds of Australian households own their own homes (about a half of whom do not have a mortgage), about a quarter rent privately and only 5 per cent live in public or community housing.

We can see that high prices squeeze out new buyers in favour of those buying second homes or apartments to rent. The figures show that, overall, home ownership has begun to decline as more people own more property; there is now a generation that can only afford to rent. In 1960, young owners (under 35) made up 60 per cent of home owners, a figure that now stands at around 45 per cent; and within that group, owners under 25 have declined from about 38 per cent to around 25 per cent. So those older than 35 have increased as a percentage of owners, and the largest increase is in those who are older than 55. In other words, those who bought before the tax and housing policies altered have gained, while those looking to buy since those changes have lost out.

Rents have also increased by comparable amounts, but the highest increases have been at the lower end of the market. The amount of public and community housing (the latter largely constituted from sales of public housing to housing associations) has remained steady, but in relation to the rise in population it has fallen by around 25 per cent. There is some rent assistance, which is capped and conditional, for those on social security. There are also various federal and state grants towards building social and affordable housing, but these scarcely compensate for the lack of commitment to the provision of affordable housing. While the rich and older generations have gained through these changes, the poor and younger generations have, systematically, become further disadvantaged.

Tax and economic policy

A post-war housing boom occurred in the US, helped by a thriving mortgage market fuelling construction. At this time, help was given via New Deal reforms whereby the Federal National Mortgage Association, often called 'Fannie May', guaranteed bank loans, thus enabling the mortgage market to take off. By the mid-1950s, 40 per cent of mortgages were federally subsidized. In the UK, and throughout Europe, the state engaged in massive construction schemes to repair and replace war-damaged housing, providing state housing and help for private ownership. Specialist mortgage finance cooperatives were encouraged to lend money, though they remained conservative in their lending habits.

By the end of the 1960s, state building programmes, as we have seen, started to be wound down, but encouragement for private ownership was stepped up, fuelling house price rises.

Laxer regulations allowed for less conservative lending by banks and specialist mortgage lenders. From the 1950s, in the UK, US and Australia, the relative cost of property taxes decreased, encouraging larger houses and helping fuel property prices. A study of 19 countries in a 25-year period from 1980 to 2005 shows that financial deregulation further fuelled mortgage lending, leading to an increase in house prices of 30 per cent. Other studies find similar results.

The global financial crisis of 2008 was caused in part by US government housing policy and its regulation of the financial system. As the Clinton government made home ownership for the poor its main policy goal, targets for lending to the poor encouraged creativity in interpreting rules governing lending and the practice of selling on debt to other banks, leading to less oversight overall. Increasing leverage and risk building occurred through the financial and banking markets. The bubble burst, and a massive rise in interest and lending rates saw many people lose their homes.

This came about as, throughout the world, finance and tax policies favour home owners over renters. Their tax benefits include tax exemptions on the asset value of their residence, which biases investment decisions; tax relief linked to the costs of home ownership, such as tax credit or deductions allowed on mortgage interest payments; and the exemption of capital gains from tax. Land appreciation is not recognized for tax purposes in the US, for example, unlike other forms of investment, because it does not provide a physical but an imputed income source. All these provisions mean that home owners benefit in ways that renters do not. In 2008, for example, the US federal government, for every dollar spent on assistance to low-income renters, spent $6 assisting home owners. And Australia operates a negative-gearing policy that encourages the rich to buy properties, even if they remain empty, as part of their investment portfolio.

Economists have long recognized and bemoaned this bias towards home owners on various economic and welfare grounds. First, on the grounds of neutrality: the system favours some more than others. Second, equity: these tax incentives are unfair and advantage the better off. Finally, they are economically inefficient: encouraging home ownership ties up economic resources, biases investment towards non-productive property, and discourages geographical and hence labour market mobility. Furthermore, price volatility can lead to macroeconomic instability – as the Global Financial Crisis (GFC) amply demonstrated. Home-ownership bias also has major distributional consequences, since it disproportionally benefits higher-income taxpayers, who would otherwise be subject to higher marginal tax rates. And it generates homelessness. These bad effects have been recognized at least as far back as the 1970s; the solutions reside in standard economics textbooks.

It is clear that reforming these tax biases would raise tax revenues, without adverse effects on income inequality or work incentives. Simulating changing home-ownership tax bias under various scenarios, across six different European countries with rather different levels of home ownership, housing market characteristics, levels of inequality and variation in the specific biases towards home ownership, promises few deleterious effects and big welfare gains. By removing bias, the tax system becomes equitable, showing a small inequality-reducing effect, a small increase in tax revenue and no effect on labour market incentives. In fact, shifting tax away from labour market revenue to investment revenue in this manner increases labour market incentives, so taxing imputed rent can increase work incentives.

In other words, the underlying cause of homelessness in the developed world is those tax incentives that governments give to home owners and investors, and which they have increased and strengthened over the past 40 years. The other side of the coin is governments' abrogation of responsibility for directly building, maintaining and renting properties to those badly off. Shifting responsibility to the private sector has meant fewer houses, especially affordable ones, being built, and has left an underclass of homeless families. Alongside changes in health provision for the mentally ill and a system that rewards those who fight addiction when homeless, rather than providing homes in order to help people fight addiction (both also driven by government), these factors have produced an increase in the number of rough sleepers and a consequent welfare loss to the whole community.

The Finnish experience

Many countries are looking to Finland for answers, at least to the most obvious housing problems. Recently developed policies there have massively reduced rough sleeping. In the 1980s, homelessness was highlighted as a serious social problem in Finland. In 1987, 1,370 families and 17,110 single people were recorded as homeless within a broad definition of that phrase. By 2008, the social housing programme and homelessness services had reduced that to 300 families and to 7,690 single people – that is, around 0.2 per cent of the population. This in itself was a success. Finland, though, still suffers problems familiar to most countries, with the high cost of housing in major cities (notably Helsinki) making it hard for younger people to enter the private housing market.

By 2004, previously steep falls in the lone adult homeless population had stalled, and it remained static at around 7,750 people. Analysis showed that these were mainly long-term homeless people with high support needs. In response, the government adopted a new approach: Paavo. What was important in Paavo was that it integrated various government agencies at local and national level, with regard to housing, mental health and drug and alcohol abuse; but it also adopted a 'housing first' policy. That is, you first find accommodation for those with psychological problems, drug or alcohol addiction, and then you try to help them. The UK, for example, takes the opposite line: finding housing for a rough sleeper is a reward for keeping off drugs or alcohol. Paavo I was designed to halve the numbers of homeless single adults within three years, using refurbished units. While it failed to meet its target, it nevertheless reduced homeless numbers by 28 per cent.

Paavo's second phase, also lasting three years, shifted the approach by making use of social rented stock and aimed to prevent people becoming homeless in the first place by examining the hidden homeless. This policy further reduced homelessness by a quarter, and analysis showed no more than 5–10 per cent experience recurrent homelessness: that is, became homeless after being helped. Finland has not achieved zero levels of homelessness, and indeed that might not be possible.

In the third phase, Paavo is developing an action plan for preventing homelessness. This looks at gender issues, youth homelessness and migrant homelessness. The gender dimension occurs because women are more likely to be part of the hidden homeless community. Particular problems occur for the young, who may leave home following abuse or difficulties with family; while migrants are often unaware of the help and entitlements that are available. Again, the plan involves integration, working across social, health, welfare, employment and social housing services.

The Finnish government acted, having consulted experts across the globe, and learning the lessons of success and failure from other countries. The Finnish approach does not seek to locate the causes of homelessness in structure or individual, but tries to meet everyone's individual needs. It emphasizes the roles of low income and debt, and tries to intervene early when housing debt arrears are low and so can be dealt with more easily, with simple schemes to avert eviction.

No one claims the Finnish scheme is perfect, but it has shown that simple measures of social housing, working with the private rented market, integrating welfare and housing needs and fast early intervention − preventing homelessness rather than responding to it − can reduce homelessness to what might be considered 'natural' levels: that is, low levels that, perhaps, given human frailty, we cannot expect to improve upon.

Final word

Over the past 40 years or so, governments have done many things that have impacted upon housing. They removed rent controls, ended subsidies and stopped building low-cost housing; they have allowed publicly owned housing to go into the private sector and not be replaced; they have provided incentives to buy property, thus pushing up house prices and creating a new rentier class with no real incentives to ensure their property is never left empty.

These housing and fiscal policies have induced house price inflation that makes it difficult not only for those on low incomes, but also for many young people in what are normally considered to be well-paid jobs, to get a foot on the bottom rung of the housing ladder. It pays investors to buy property not just to let to those needing a home, but as a 'second home', or to rent out for holidays or via Airbnb for parties. Thus those with homes bought with the help of tax subsidies may also have their holiday accommodation subsidized by taxpayers. Fiscal policy is such, in some countries, that it is even worthwhile buying property to leave vacant, since gains can be made by house price inflation. At the same time as the low-rent private rental market is being squeezed in this manner, government has stopped building low-rent properties itself. Governments outrageously blame the homeless for the situation they have directly created. The responsibility for homelessness in the developed world − no matter what its level and distribution − is to be laid fairly and squarely at the door of governments and the policies they have pursued in the past 40 years.

5

Problem Gambling

Most people gamble – or at least like to have the occasional flutter – and gambling is a problem for a relatively small percentage of them. In the US, around 80 per cent of the population are estimated to gamble at least once a year, while problem gambling is estimated to affect only about 3–5 per cent. Australia has more of a gambling culture than the US or the UK. While some estimates put the problem in Australia at a higher level than in the US (5–7 per cent), most studies suggest problem gambling is much lower: 0.5–2 per cent, with a further 2 per cent at some risk of developing a problem.

The variation in these estimates is due to the different sources they come from. Some figures arise from surveys where gamblers fill in questionnaires about their habits. Their answers are assessed to judge whether they have a problem or not – but the questions might be weighted in different ways. For example, the US *Diagnostic and Statistical Manual of Mental Disorders* defines pathological gambling as the 'chronic inability to refrain from gambling to an extent that causes serious disruption to core life aspects such as career, health and family'. If someone agrees with five or more of the following statements, they are defined as a pathological gambler:

- You have often gambled longer than you had planned.
- You have often gambled until your last dollar was gone.
- Thoughts of gambling have caused you to lose sleep.
- You have used your income or savings to gamble while letting bills go unpaid.

- You have made repeated, unsuccessful attempts to stop gambling.
- You have broken the law or considered breaking the law to finance your gambling.
- You have borrowed money to finance your gambling.
- You have felt depressed or suicidal because of your gambling losses.
- You have been remorseful after gambling.
- You have gambled to get money to meet your financial obligations.

However, people might be considered to have problems with gambling even if they do not admit to five of these statements. For that reason, some make a distinction between 'problem gambling' – seen as a pathological condition – and 'gambling problems', where gambling has led to troubles within one's household. I will not consider this particular issue further, but simply note that some gambling problems are sufficiently bad that they are recognized as a medical condition, indeed an addiction.

Many people gamble; only a few choose to do so recklessly. Given that relatively few suffer problems as a result of their gambling, we might think that governments are right to say that problem gambling is an issue of personal responsibility. Certainly, governments do look to individual responsibility in this area. While sports programmes on Australian television constantly refer to the betting odds available, they also constantly remind people to bet responsibly, as indeed do advertisements placed by the gambling industry. So, government does look to individuals to behave responsibly and provides encouragement for them to do so. It also works with the gambling industry to try to ensure that the industry acts responsibly towards its customers. However, governments also recognize that gambling problems can result from pathological or addictive behaviour. As such, they are seen as a medical problem that is beyond the immediate control of individuals and hence lies outside the scope of individual responsibility. This chapter examines the relationship between the responsibilities of government, industry and individuals for gambling problems.

Changes over time

Governments once regulated gambling more strictly than most do today, some countries more than others. The justification for such strict regulation was not directly related to the well-being of the public; it was moral or religious. Gambling was regarded as morally wrong, a sign of vicious not virtuous behaviour. To be sure, governments were aware of the dangers that gambling poses to families. The offspring of the rich squandering the family fortune by gambling it away on the horses or at cards was a favourite trope of Victorian novels and the subject of popular paintings. Important personages being blackmailed by foreign agents because of gambling debts later became a standard plot line in novels. Meanwhile, the poverty of the lower classes was often portrayed as the result of their immorality, of which gaming was a major component.

Gambling was essentially outlawed in the US in the early 20th century, largely by state law. Legalization in Nevada in 1931 caused it to become the gambling capital of the country. In 1976, New Jersey legalized gambling in Atlantic City, now the second major city for casinos. As in other countries, tight restrictions pushed gambling underground, to be controlled by criminal organizations. Hence, a convincing case could eventually be developed to relax the regulations to encourage less criminalized gambling activities. There was also a realization that the government was losing a source of tax revenue by driving gambling underground, and that opening casinos, for example, could revitalize local economies. State lotteries started appearing, in part to discourage illegal lotteries, and by 2018 the annual spend was $77 billion on 47 state lotteries.

The UK saw similarly strict regulation of gambling during the 20th century. Casinos were highly regulated, betting shops ('turf accountants') were subject to detailed legislation to reduce their attractiveness and betting was tightly controlled: slot machines and other arcade betting machines could only operate in certain settings and winnings were limited. High-stakes betting was essentially an illegal activity carried on behind closed doors or only in special parts of the very few casinos that operated. For much of the 20th century, the most popular forms of betting were on horses or dogs in betting shops or at race tracks and, for the broader population, the 'football pools', in which successful predictions for the outcomes of matches attracted relatively high pay-outs. From the 1980s onwards, the UK's very strict controls were relaxed. Betting shops were allowed to become more welcoming, more licences for casinos were granted, a national lottery was established and slot machines could pay out higher sums.

State lotteries are often defended on the grounds that the revenues will go to good causes such as education or health or will support charitable and local organizations. They have the unintended effect of being a regressive form of raising state revenue, since overwhelmingly it is poorer people who buy lottery tickets. Thus the poor at times are unwittingly subsidizing the activities of the more affluent (the UK National Lottery, for example, has provided funds for opera and theatre companies) or replacing state funding (many US state lotteries help pay for educational needs).

Australia provides a contrast to the moralistic and prohibitive practices of the US and the UK, having long had a relatively liberal approach to gambling. Betting is regarded as a traditional national pastime. It took place largely at race tracks, though illegal betting occurred, especially as radio and then television took off. To combat this, state governments introduced Totalisator Agency Boards (TABs), and by the 1970s betting was the most popular type of gambling, generating large revenues for state governments. Betting on sports was illegal until the 1980s, and in the 1990s other forms of gambling were legalized. The privatization of TABs began in 1994 with the sale of TAB Victoria, with other states following; the Australian Capital Territory (ACT) did not privatize till 2014, while Western Australia announced plans to privatize in 2019. The first Australian casino was opened in Tasmania in 1973, and there were casinos in all the states by the end of the 1990s. There have been state lotteries from the early 20th century, and a private lottery, Tattslotto, has operated for over 50 years. Today there are more than half a dozen major lotteries, most of which have now moved online.

Australia is different to many other countries because of the impact of electronic gaming machines (EGMs). First introduced in 1956, and licensed for use in community venues such as clubs and hotels in order to generate revenue for improved facilities for members, their popularity soared from the 1980s. Poker machines ('pokies') are the most common type, and today all the states have legalized them, apart from Western Australia (which does, however, have cashless video-lottery terminals). Expenditure on pokies soon exceeded that on other forms of gambling. There are now around 200,000 EGMs in Australia: about 11 machines for every 1,000 Australians. Although they are played regularly by less than 5 per cent of the population, EGMs are thought to be the source of around 80 per cent of gambling problems – and the source of about 50–60 per cent of national gambling revenue.

This claim is somewhat problematic, since demonstrating causation is always difficult in social science research. The complication is that problem gamblers rarely engage in only one form of gambling. So most of the research shows that when EGM participation is run in a statistical model with all the other forms of gambling and some basic demographics, EGM play, along with sports betting and casino table games, remains significant. That only *suggests* causation. However, it is known that the mechanisms that lead to gambling addiction make EGMs particularly dangerous.

Australia has enacted responsible-gambling legislation to guide state government policies. It imposes greater constraints on the industry than in the US, but grants greater autonomy than in most European countries. Some states/territories have mandatory codes of practice (the Northern Territory, South Australia, ACT and Tasmania); others have non-mandatory and voluntary codes. Rules govern the advertising and provision of products, and the availability of cash terminals, the access of minors and the sale of alcohol in venues. Staff must also undergo approved responsible-gambling training. But even mandatory guidelines are not always followed, particularly at smaller venues.

Gambling is a major source of revenue for governments – particularly for state governments in the US and Australia. Furthermore, in Australia, EGMs are part of the culture of the clubs that form the membership base of political parties. So there is a direct party-political interest in allowing EGMs, since they form an important source of revenue for political parties. For this reason, governments in Australia have been reluctant to directly regulate gambling. Rather, they intervene through funding research, writing reports and encouraging gambling organizations to self-regulate through identifying and helping pathological gamblers.

The justification of strict betting laws had been public morality, not public welfare, and when gambling restrictions began to be eased across the world from the 1970s onwards, the reasoning was that it is not the job of the state to enforce morality. It was further argued that, for most people, gambling is a harmless activity. Making access to legal gambling easier opened up a harmless pastime for many people and removed a set of activities from the realm of victimless crimes. While it is generally recognized in the liberal democratic West that it is not the government's job to enforce morality, and that gambling is a minor and harmless activity for most people, it also has to be acknowledged that the easing of gambling restrictions has resulted in the public suffering from a greater degree of problem gambling.

Gambling is an interesting topic for this book. Once governments accepted it was not their job to regulate their citizens' morality, it was incumbent upon them to relax prohibitive gambling restrictions. If people wanted to gamble, then that was their responsibility. In some ways, gambling could be taken as a paradigm for responsible choice. Every bet has an associated risk, and what is free choice if it does not include taking responsibility for the benefits and costs associated with the choices one makes? These costs and benefits can be seen in terms of the risks associated with choices. Gambling is a process where the risks can be more easily quantified than in many other choices. Of course, everyone ought to know that the house always wins (it is a business, after all), so in the long run one is likely to lose. However, if there is some enjoyment to be had in the gambling itself, that 'loss' is simply a payment for pleasure, just as we pay for other pleasures, such as fine dining or theatre-going. And we might be prepared to pay reasonable amounts of our income not only for the simple pleasure of gambling, but also to have that chance to gain riches beyond those attainable from our normal occupations.

However, some research suggests that the enjoyment from gambling is not quite like the enjoyment from other sources of pleasure. Typically, people pay for entertainment because they value the product more than their money, and this makes sense in terms of their stated pleasure after experiencing the entertainment. They are happier than they were before they paid the money. However, in gambling we find that on average people do not feel any different after they pay the money: that is, they gain no extra pleasure from gambling. Perhaps this is unsurprising, since we tend to think of gambling pleasure purely in terms of monetary gain or loss. The research suggests that the thrill of the anticipation tends to make up for the fact that there is a house edge. Nevertheless, though there is some pleasure to be gained in gambling other than the possibility of financial gain, gambling ranks low as a form of pure entertainment – perhaps similar to supporting a perennially disappointing sports team.

In terms of how responsibility was discussed in the opening chapter, then, gambling is a paradigm activity for government to say to its citizens: the choice is yours, you take responsibility for the outcomes given your actions. You can see the risks, you can weigh the alternatives, what you spend is entirely up to you. The only role for government in this individual responsibility model is to ensure that the house does not cheat.

On the other hand, it is increasingly being recognized that gambling problems, for at least some people, are pathological. Gambling is a form of addiction; that means problem gambling is something that requires medical attention and psychological help. As a pathology or addiction, the behaviour is, by definition, outside of the control of individuals and so not rightly part of their individual responsibility. Pathologies are things for which we recognize we cannot easily assign personal responsibility. Problem gambling thus seems to be an issue where government ought to step in and help people. Indeed, as we shall see, government does do this to some extent. It does take some responsibility for the results of its own regulatory processes, though it also tries to shift some responsibility to other agents.

Gamblers and their problems

First we need to examine problem gambling and see how far gambling problems are indeed pathological and constitute a genuine addiction. Estimates of how many people gamble vary. In part, as we have seen, that is because most of the evidence comes from surveys: however carefully worded the questions, not all respondents will interpret them in the same way. Does buying a raffle ticket at the church bazaar count? Usually not, but each gambling survey tends to have a different conception of what it considers gambling, and they do not always provide the same advice to respondents, so we cannot be sure what respondents think of as gambling. Usually the questions are directed at gambling in more organized forms; still, most people would regard buying a national lottery ticket as very different from visiting a casino or gambling through internet forums. Nevertheless, some estimates suggest that over 80 per cent of American adults gamble at least once a year.

While relatively small numbers – between 3 and 7 per cent across the US, UK and Australia – are considered to be problem gamblers, it is also claimed that gambling is problematic for larger numbers of people. Gambling problems are not evenly spread across the population: the young (the 18–35 age group), males, lower socio-economic groups and people not in stable relationships suffer higher rates of problems. Indigenous peoples also seem to have higher rates of problem gambling, as do ethnic minorities (defined as those who do not speak the country's dominant language at home).

One of the issues that bedevils the literature on gambling problems is actually defining what the nature of these problems is. Many writers make a distinction between gambling problems – that is, difficulties for a household or individual that might be short lived – and problem gamblers, who have long-term psychological issues with gambling. This distinction relies upon the problem gamblers displaying psychological markers and pathological behaviour absent from those whose gambling has caused them temporary problems, and is contested by some observers.

Rather than delve into detailed disputes on definitions, I shall concentrate here on the elements of the problem that are mostly widely agreed upon. I shall also outline some of the evidence about the ways in which changing regulations have affected how widespread gambling problems have become. There is, in fact, massive controversy in the scientific literature about both the psychological problems associated with problem gamblers and the effects of regulatory changes. Not only is the issue difficult to study, but it is also, despite not being in the public eye too much, exceedingly politically contentious.

Who defines problem gambling?

The vast majority of gambling research is funded by the gambling industry itself. This does not necessarily mean that all such industry-funded research is not high quality, for some of it at least is published in widely respected journals subject to independent peer review. However, it does mean that the research agenda – the sort of research that is conducted, the questions addressed – is affected by the industry's own interests. And, of course, the peer review assessors will themselves be academics who work on gambling and are likely to receive much of their funding from the industry, and thus are implicated in the gambling industry's agenda themselves.

While most gambling research is indirectly funded by the gambling industry, state or national governments do also fund research, and some is independent. This maintains some level of independence, but governments will tend to publish what is politically palatable. Certainly there are hosts of research reports that remain unpublished, much to the chagrin of some gambling researchers. There are also some major controversies over academics who take (or refuse) research money from the gambling industry. In Australia some organizations such as Clubs ACT and Clubs NSW have made claims about who they think provide 'sensible gambling research', which is controversial, particularly since they have funded specific gambling research laboratories and not others.

While the gambling industry undoubtedly has an interest in ensuring that problem gambling does not get too far out of hand, lest the public make demands for regulation that government cannot ignore, it also has an interest in defining and studying it in particular ways. Meanwhile, the industry knows more about how to extract the highest profits from their gambling machines than regulators do. Bluntly put, the industry knows how to make those susceptible to gambling addiction become addicted. It is in its interest to encourage addiction, even if, once someone is addicted, it is prepared to help ensure that the addiction can be controlled.

Furthermore, even where governments fund gambling research, they are known to embargo some of the findings. In many jurisdictions around the world, gambling provides large revenues for state, national or federal governments, so while governments may be willing to deal with the social issues that arise from gambling problems, they want to avoid addressing those issues in a way that deleteriously affects their income stream. In Australia, for example, political parties (especially Labor) enjoy a large revenue stream from the EGMs in their clubs, and therefore have a direct pecuniary interest in the regulations that are instituted at both state and federal level. Local governments, too, see advantages in locating casinos in their jurisdiction, as they can be a draw for tourists – although the benefits are diluted if too many local governments permit casinos.

The gambling industry contributes substantially to the Liberal Party in the form of donations. The 2017 Tasmanian election was a case in point. Tatts group helped the Liberal Party with a pro-personal responsibility line – and claims that removing EGMs would wreck the service economy and amateur sports. They spent millions to ensure that the Labor Party did not get in. So essentially, both parties are vulnerable to the gambling industry.

The other problem is that state governments are divided, while the gambling industry is largely composed of national conglomerates. The divide-and-conquer logic behind the gambling industry's public affairs strategy puts states at a collective disadvantage, and is one of the reasons why the federal government is increasingly interested in taking in parts of gambling regulation for itself, including regulation of online gambling.

Third, when it comes to the issues concerned with pathological gambling, the research agenda, reasonably enough, is determined by the medical profession, whose major interest is in helping people with severe gambling problems. Their interest is not determined by a carefully controlled scientific analysis of what determines problem gambling. After all, the same behavioural attributes might have different causes. The neurological evidence of addiction, including gambling addiction, is complex. For all these reasons, the science needs to be handled with even more care than the evidence we have seen in other areas in earlier chapters.

Having said that, we can make too much of such disputes. Debate often concerns issues at the margins of the problem. Most experts will agree on the vast bulk of people who are problem gamblers, disagreeing only on marginal cases. And many of the disputes about the best way of handling gambling problems may come about because the multi-causal attributes of the problem are not given sufficient weight.

Addiction or personal responsibility?

With those warnings in place, can we say what constitutes gambling problems and what constitutes addiction and problem gambling? The American Psychological Association, in DSM-IV, defines pathological gambling as 'persistent and recurrent maladaptive gambling behaviour, characterized by an inability to control gambling, leading to significant deleterious psychosocial consequences: personal, familial, financial, professional and legal'. In this way, problem gambling is distinguished from gambling problems, the latter being a broader category of financial difficulties or household frictions that are created through some aspect of gambling behaviour, and tend to be less severe and less long-lasting.

Problem gambling can be thought of as an addiction. While there are various competing definitions of gambling addiction – as with problem gambling – we do know that there are neurological symptoms that are associated with problem gambling. Furthermore, there is strong behavioural and neurological evidence that pathological gambling and substance dependence share a common set of features. These indicators are very similar to those found in other forms of addiction, such as alcohol or drug addiction. Since, in gambling, they are presented without any form of external chemical stimulus, gambling addiction can be seen as the purest form of addiction.

We might think, therefore, that we could, at least in theory, provide a fairly straightforward account of personal responsibility for problem gambling. If genetic markers can be established for gambling addiction, then we could know how responsible someone is. We could make judgements about how difficult it is for someone to control their gambling in relation to another person (do they share the 'gambling genes' or not?). In theory, we could know the probability of distribution of problem gambling across any society if we knew the distribution of such genes and the propensity of addiction under particular gambling stimuli.

This is not the case, however. Not only is that an overly simplistic view of genetic determination, but the neurological evidence about addiction suggests that behaviour and addiction do not have a simple unifying structure and that there are multiple neurodynamical and neurochemical vulnerabilities which cut across the different types of addictions. Nevertheless, there is a core neurochemical signature that characterizes drug dependencies and pathological gambling (as well as, potentially, overeating). So, while we cannot simply read off addiction from neural dysfunction, addiction does nevertheless tend to follow a standard behavioural course, because it is a human vulnerability that has evolved in our history. This evolved vulnerability is generated by the dispositional structure of decision making, which normally serves us well. Like other addictive behaviour, these facts about its causes also help explain why people can recover from addiction. This fact is particularly important, as gambling addiction is often associated (or comorbid) with other medical and behavioural factors. Overcoming addiction can be enabled by tackling these other conditions simultaneously.

There are a number of causal factors associated with problem gambling. The first is genetic, in terms either of specific genes that confer greater vulnerability to addiction or of less direct evidence for heritability. Second, there is evidence in addicts of biochemical changes at the level of the neuron. So there is something going on at the molecular level. There is also something happening at the system level in the brain. Brain regions and circuits do not function in addicts in the same way as in others when they gamble. This affects their goal-seeking behaviour and how individuals view their own actions. It has an effect on their psychology and their cognitive functions. We also know that social and cultural factors can be very important in the development of a gambling addiction.

Some studies have suggested that if we examine different pathways, we can see different ways in which people find themselves with gambling problems. The first pathway is behavioural conditioning: this kind of problem gambler is characterized by fluctuations between regular and heavy or excessive gambling because of the effects of conditioning, distorted cognitions surrounding their probability of winning and/or a series of bad judgements or poor decisions, rather than impaired control. People in this group are often preoccupied with gambling. They often display other addictions, such as alcoholism, and exhibit high levels of depression and anxiety in response to the financial burdens their gambling creates.

The second pathway is taken by those who are emotionally vulnerable problem gamblers. Often, they display the same ecological and conditioning processes as those in the first group, but they also suffer anxiety and depression and display a history of poor coping and problem-solving skills. People on this pathway often have a troubled family background and life events. While the first set of people often gamble initially for entertainment or as part of their social group, the second are emotionally vulnerable as a result of psychosocial and biological factors. Gambling helps relieve aversive affective states by providing respite from their problems.

Those labelled 'antisocial impulsive gamblers' are on the third pathway. While displaying many of the same features as the other two groups, they are characterized by neurological or neurochemical dysfunction. Examples of dysfunction include impulsive and antisocial personality disorders and attention deficit, manifesting in severe multiple maladaptive behaviours that affect other aspects of the gambler's general social life. People in this group are also more likely to display substance abuse.

The distinction between gambling as an addiction and it being a problem lacking the neurological characteristics of addiction is important for individual help. There are good reasons for keeping the idea that there are problem gamblers without the neurological mechanisms of addiction. We do not yet fully understand the mechanisms of gambling problems and are at the prevalence estimation stage of the science. We cannot wait until the science is fully specified before we act to help those who get into difficulties. There is consensus among researchers, those who provide treatment to gamblers and indeed in the gambling industry itself, that large numbers of gamblers at least occasionally lose more money than they can comfortably afford to. A smaller number bring catastrophic problems on themselves and their families. If there is no significant qualitative difference between addicts and those who do not always control their habits, and we acknowledge that anyone can become addicted, then the gambling industry and government have an intense ethical responsibility. If there is a significant qualitative difference, then the problem is less severe, since then the distinctive pathological behaviour can be identified and sufferers excluded. That is the situation as it exists in many countries.

EGMs

Most researchers accept that EGMs are associated with the highest level of problem gambling, although the strictest tests of causal inference cannot make this case. EGMs seem to cause a faster progression to pathological gambling than more traditional forms. One study suggests they lead to pathological gambling in 1.08 years, as opposed to 3.58 years through more traditional forms of gambling.

EGMs might be the most addictive form of gambling because they have very short time intervals between placing the bet and the outcome, and they are the most continuous gambling activity possible. Each reel spin is about 3–5 seconds, and gamblers play very close to this maximum (4–10 seconds), with regular players playing faster than others. Pay-outs are also disbursed very quickly. Many EGMs are designed to resemble older mechanical versions, but of course they do not actually have spinning wheels. They will often make it look as though the player would have won if the spin had gone a little further, an appearance that can be achieved with no real effect on the probability of winning (unlike the mechanical versions). These 'near-miss' designs are beginning to fade out in new machines. The biggest driver of addictive play in EGMs is multiple pay lines. Experienced gamblers manage as many as 15 lines, but three is a standard number for beginners. Multiple lines use up cognitive resources so gamblers are less able to over-ride their addictive motivation; and they mean that the gambler wins something every time, although of course generally losing more overall. The sound and visual effects signalling that goes with winning sound constantly, thus encouraging further participation and motivating the addiction. These new designs are highly addictive and encourage problem gambling. Allowing gambling but regulating so the most addictive forms are banned ought to satisfy everyone bar the most venal gambling operators. The problem with the academic research efforts is that, paid by the gambling industry, they do not pay enough attention to some of the most important issues.

Through experimental set-ups, the industry has, in fact, discovered how to make the most money by setting the reel spins and pay-out at the optimal levels. Not too fast, to ensure that punters get the high, but fast enough to maximize the amount they will play. Addictive gamblers have been shown to get their high from playing at the moment they put their money in, not when winning or when the pay-out comes. Experiments have shown that reduced speed and sound result in decreased enjoyment and excitement, and that at the speed that is standardly set for these machines pathological gamblers find it more difficult to stop playing. Slow the play down and even pathological gamblers find it easier to walk away.

Evidence from Norway

The case of Norway offers evidence of how changing EGM regulations affected behaviours in the early part of the 21st century. During the 1990s, traditional mechanical machines were replaced with EGMs featuring high speed, light and sound reinforcements, along with banknote acceptors (so stakes could be higher) and higher pay-outs. In Norway these new machines increased gambling by an estimated factor of 47; by 2001 they accounted for 40 per cent of gross gambling turnover. Turnover continued to increase, rising by 250 per cent in the next five years and accounting for two thirds of gambling turnover in 2005. EGMs were a major source of revenue for many sports clubs, grocery stores and charities – the Norwegian Red Cross, for example, derived almost half its income from EGM gambling. Concerns about the extent and severity of problem gambling escalated. Therapists working with problem gamblers were particularly concerned with EGMs and called for restrictions on their use, while population surveys also suggested they were causing increasing problems compared with other forms of gambling. EGMs seemed to be a particular problem for young people (aged 18–35).

In response, the Norwegian government started restricting the use of EGMs. First, it banned banknote acceptors (in 2006), then prohibited slot-machine usage between midnight and 6 am. Finally, in mid-2007, EGMs were temporarily banned for a period of 18 months, before being replaced by new-style machines, now run by a government monopoly. The new EGMs were designed to be less harmful. They require a personal gambling card, enabling better enforcement of a legal age limit, and meaning that there is no cash pay-out. The card can be set to cap losses on a daily and a monthly basis. The machines have less audio-visual stimulation, and will shut down automatically if punters lose too much. While turnover from other forms of gambling increased at that time by 3 per cent, total gambling turnover fell by 17 per cent. Clearly the restrictions affected the overall amount of gambling. Given the level of problem gambling, many considered this reduction beneficial, particularly as the government provided short-term compensatory payments to charities and other organizations that lost out (using gambling tax revenue).

Norway also saw a dramatic drop in the prevalence of self-assessed problem gambling among young people (from around 6.5 per cent in 2002–8 to 4 per cent in 2009–13). In the total adult population, the prevalence of problem gambling fell from a high of 5.5 per cent in 2002 to a low of 3 per cent in 2013. Helplines dealing with gambling problems reported that EGMs being the main problem dropped from a high of 711 in 2006 to a low of just eight people in 2009, though picking up to 66 by 2012. Other types of gambling games being the main problem in that period moved from 129 in 2006 to 254 by 2012.

Norway subsequently liberalized again; in 2014 the state lottery launched new internet-based games, including casino games, bingo and scratch cards, and from 2015 allowed poker tournaments in private homes and national poker tournaments.

What Norway's changing regulation of EGMs shows is that it is possible to regulate gambling games with important effects on gamblers, particularly – in this case – young ones. Since most adult problem gamblers started their addiction when young, these results could be important for dealing with problem gambling.

Regulation

The gambling industry is not regulated like other businesses. Governments tend to ensure that large gambling concerns demonstrate that they have substantial resources, sufficient to pay out to gamblers. They must also demonstrate that they are competent and trustworthy. There is no particular reason why gambling concerns should need to do this more than other companies; probably the historical association with criminal organizations lies behind the felt need. Moreover, demanding such proofs may undercut potential critics who want to end gambling as a legitimate business enterprise.

Governments also scrutinize gambling machines and casinos, since gambling is a concern where it is relatively easy for firms to cheat their customers without their knowledge. Governments also tax gambling to a greater extent than other products or services. This is sometimes justified on the grounds of controlling profits and reducing the amount of gambling, but neither reason can withstand much scrutiny. Rather, it is because taxing the gambling industry is a relatively popular way of raising revenue. Only gamblers are affected, and it is relatively hidden from view.

One of the main political problems from a regulatory point of view is that the significant revenue that governments gain from a thriving gambling industry effectively makes citizens shareholders in the industry. While gambling tax rates have tended to fall in the past 30 years, revenue has increased. Gambling taxation is regressive, and increasingly so as more liberal gambling laws have broadened access to gambling. Governments therefore have a vested interest in ensuring a strong gambling industry; as such they are more reluctant to regulate in ways that might affect numbers of gamblers and industry profits.

We might think that gambling ought to be left to market forces in much the same way as other businesses. After all, that would endow people with responsibility for their choices, and free markets do seem to supply the goods that people want. Competition would also open up more businesses and perhaps improve the odds of winning. However, if anyone could start a gambling business, anyone could organize a lottery for personal profit. And that would reduce the ability of governments to run lotteries for good causes. Bookmakers could take odds on all sorts of things, including school and college sporting events, the future price of stocks, and so on. This could lead to all these types of events becoming vulnerable to cheating, bias and so on, as people try to beat the odds. This could destroy many types of social activities and ruin the enjoyment of people who do not want to gamble. Completely open and free gambling on anything could have massive negative externalities for society.

Another claim is that EGM revenue goes back to the community via contributions to the community. What this means in practice varies. In Australia, for example, poker machine operators must set aside a certain percentage of their income to give back to the community. Clubs must then show how that money is spent in their annual reports. However, exactly what constitutes a public good is a malleable concept – clubs often define the club itself as a public good, spending most of the money on operating costs and refurbishment of their own venue. When they invest in or sponsor local sport, clubs tend to prefer the glory of bringing in professional or semi-professional sportspeople to play for the team affiliated with the club, rather than putting money into coaching or developing sports. So again, we might be sceptical about the money going back into the community in the form of public goods.

If gambling machines were allowed everywhere – from pubs and clubs to shops, cafes and street corners – it would be very difficult to regulate them and ensure they operated fairly, as well as making it hard to deal with problem gambling. Indeed, the Norwegian experience suggests that stricter regulations would help problem gamblers. Specifically, ensuring that people need a personal gambling card in order to gamble on EGMs, online or in casinos would enable problem gamblers to be more easily identified and given help, while not stopping those who like to gamble for pleasure. That would be the most efficient way to help those who cannot take personal responsibility, while allowing people who can gamble responsibly to do so.

Online gambling is another area of concern. It is often claimed that governments cannot regulate online gambling since overseas entities can offer services that break domestic laws. One of the problems is that countries have tended to make domestic laws for online gambling so tough that domestic suppliers cannot compete. But the idea that it is impossible to regulate online gambling is not entirely true, since there are many international agreements over trade, including other internet provisions. International agreements can be made, as they are for other types of internet providers; and while these agreements cannot entirely stop people from avoiding regulatory processes, they do generally work in other areas. They would, at least, force people to make a choice to use the internet illegally. We do not refuse to regulate in other areas of life simply because implementation is not 100 per cent effective. Again, personal gambling cards could be used for domestic online gambling systems.

Governments can also regulate pay-outs for national and other lotteries. While massive pay-outs encourage punters, limiting headline pay-out and increasing the number of winners sharing smaller amounts would still allow lotteries to operate and would spread the enjoyment and rewards. Governments should refrain from using lotteries to fund regular public goods and services, and direct profits to specialist 'extras', such as supporting charities. As indicated earlier, though, we need to be careful about what kinds of 'extras' these are. The process could be democratized by, for example, the local community suggesting how revenue should be spent locally and voting for it in referendums or other forms of participation. When lotteries replace regular taxation they are regressive in nature.

As in other areas, governments cannot avoid responsibility for the number of problem gamblers, nor for their distribution, which tends to be among poorer, less educated and marginal groups. Addictive gambling behaviour is also associated with other forms of addiction. We know that liberalizing gambling has created more problem gamblers. In itself, this is not a sufficient reason for not liberalizing. Many people derive harmless pleasure from gambling, and it is an industry that employs many people. When it was highly regulated, illegal betting was rife. Regulating and making gambling mainstream can help governments to control some of the problems associated with gambling – the ease of cheating customers, gambling establishments going bust or closing shop owing money, as well as customers getting into financial difficulty. If such difficulties arise through illegal activity, it is harder for people to seek help.

Nevertheless, governments need to recognize – and, to be fair, most have done so – that problem gambling is a medical condition and that most, if not all, those who fall into serious financial difficulties through gambling are suffering pathological behaviours and are not fully responsible for their actions. Governments can work with the gambling industry, but self-regulation is not going to be sufficient. Governments can do more, particularly in relation to the earlier identification of problem gamblers and developing appropriate interventions.

We should acknowledge, however, that so far there have been no demonstrably effective treatments for problem gambling. The literature is stuck in a mire of potentials and trials with mixed results. Most studies do not show gambling treatments to be effective beyond a year. This is partly due to budget constraints on the studies with not enough follow-up research, but the suspicion is that researchers are publishing the best-case scenarios, which is why they do not include long-term results. Some studies suggest there is no difference between people in treatment for problem gambling and those who are not. There is widespread acknowledgement that something must be done, however, and funding gambling counselling services has been part of this effort.

Unfortunately, although governments are morally obliged to address a problem they directly helped create, counselling services do not appear to achieve the objective of reducing gambling harm. As with approaches to other addictions, harm reduction is now widely seen as more feasible than outright prevention. Researchers are in the process of developing healthy gambling guidelines, as governments have done with alcohol. If we accept that governments should do something, then perhaps a more useful allocation of resources might effectively become moral licensing – putting gambling revenue to good use elsewhere – even if a small section of the population is harmed.

Final word

This book has explored a number of case studies demonstrating that governments are responsible for the patterns of problems in various policy areas and should not, therefore, attempt to shift the blame to individuals for their condition, and thence for the pattern itself. Gambling is an instance where it is widely recognized that some of the problems we see are not attributable to the people who suffer them. It thus provides a nice intersection where the personal and the political are implicated.

Governments once regulated gambling far more than they do now. Their reasons were moral and paternalistic. Deregulation can be justified and, in the main, is to the advantage of most people, since many people like to gamble occasionally. However, deregulation has created a set of problem gamblers. We should recognize that gambling is a form of addiction that causes welfare loss not only to the problem gamblers themselves, but also to their families. We should be aware that the gambling industry itself has conducted large amounts of research into what makes their products appealing. They know precisely how to get people addicted.

I have mentioned some of the political difficulties involved in increasing regulation on gambling. First, research is dominated by the gambling industry and by government itself; both have some interest in nurturing a profitable gambling industry and so are reluctant to intervene too much. This is not to disparage all the research that is done, but there are suggestions that some research avoids addressing certain questions, specifically over the design of EGMs and the nature of services provided in casinos.

Governments generally raise a lot of money through gambling taxation, which is a relatively popular form of taxation, and in some countries, notably Australia, the political parties themselves raise substantial funds from EGMs in their clubs.

The orientation of the industry-led research is into 'responsible gambling'. The responsible gambling paradigm has also been taken up by government. However, this has led to a neglect of the social consequences of harms to non-problem gamblers. While we cannot assume that simply because the gambling industry makes large profits from non-problem gamblers those gamblers are losing welfare – since they might be gaining pleasure from the gambling act itself. However, the profits from non-problem gamblers swamp those from problem gamblers suggesting that there might well be large consumer welfare losses.

Gambling is an interesting topic, since we might think that we can demand that individuals accept responsibility for their gambling behaviour. However, neurological studies show that addictive behaviour occurs when the brain's rewards system goes awry. A process that delivers evolutionary advantages most of the time can, under certain pressures not encountered 'naturally', lead to pathological behaviours. In these cases, we cannot assign the type of responsibility – control – that we expect. Here the regulators who allow the activity to be available must take responsibility for its effects on the population. Governments are responsible for the degree of problem gambling among their populations.

For this reason, governments should recognize the problem they have in part caused and regulate the gambling industry. That can mean working with the gambling industry to impose restrictions on those who are addicted, and also to offer direct assistance to problem gamblers. As we have seen in this chapter, there is evidence that government can make a big difference with some strict regulations. To be sure, some gamblers might evade them by going online, but that is no reason for government not to act and help the many.

6

Recreational Drugs Policy

Much of this book has been arguing that government has reneged on its responsibility to its citizens by claiming, in the name of liberty, that they need to take responsibility for what happens to them. I have maintained that, generally speaking, citizens cannot be held responsible for many of the bad social outcomes which we witness in society today. Individuals can only be held responsible for the choices they make given the situation in which they find themselves. Government is largely responsible for their situation. I have also argued that there are certain features about human biology that mean we know that people will tend to respond to certain sorts of incentives. Government should be aware of those responses and, rather than simply throwing blame or responsibility on to individuals, it ought to design policy that helps people.

This chapter is about drugs policy. In the main it is about recreational drugs, but occasionally I will also contrast the manner in which government designs and implements policies on recreational drugs with how it deals with drugs produced for medical purposes – what I will refer to as 'medical drugs'. While governments are keen not to be too paternalistic in many fields, their attitudes to recreational drugs are highly paternalistic. We can contrast recreational drug policies with gambling, where the paternalistic policies of the past have given way to a more libertarian outlook. In the main, this has been welcome, but it has created a bigger class of problem gamblers. I argued that government needs to recognize that a large degree of problem gambling results from liberalization and it needs to take responsibility for that, particularly noting that addiction deprives an individual of full responsibility for their actions. Government must acknowledge its duty to help problem gamblers, especially since their problem has deleterious effects not only for themselves but also their families.

Governments are still paternalistic when it comes to recreational drugs. Most recreational drugs are criminalized, in producing, selling, buying or consuming – sometimes in all aspects. The majority of those who work in drugs policy – not only academics doing research, but also many who work in the field with addicts, as well as many senior police officers, public servants and, often privately, politicians – believe that the criminalization of recreational drugs is a failed public policy. They do not agree on where we should go, but most believe that we should relax the more stringent penalties for drug users.

In the past 30 years, largely because drugs policy is viewed as a failure by many relevant actors, some governments around the world have started to gently liberalize recreational drug policy. In the main this involves the decriminalization or legalization of certain types of drugs, such as cannabis. (Decriminalization means it is not a crime to be in possession of or to take drugs, though it might be a civil offence; legalization makes it legal to produce and sell drugs.) Sometimes this relaxation of policy covers medical use only, sometimes also recreational purposes. Other countries have gone further. Portugal, notably, has decriminalized all drug use. Precisely what that means and what effect it has had on Portugal's population I will consider below. Of course, some recreational drugs such as alcohol and tobacco are not criminalized, although they are regulated. Tobacco regulation, given the evidence of the damage to the health not only of consumers but also of those subject to secondary smoke, has been severely tightened in recent years. In this chapter I want to consider why the state is paternalistic with regard to recreational drugs, yet not in other policy areas.

Drug use

The stated justification for criminalizing drug use is paternalistic and moralistic. The standard arguments include: drug use is harmful to the users; drug users are less economically productive and have higher health costs; drug use increases public spending; drug users harm others; drug users are more likely to commit other criminal acts to feed the drug use; drug use upsets non-users; drug use is contagious and some people, especially the young, need to be protected from exposure. Lord Windlesham, opening the second reading of the UK Misuse of Drugs Act 1971 in the House of Lords, said that the guiding principle of the government was that it could legislate to restrict liberties which threaten society and human welfare. That is a pretty weighty defence of criminalization of recreational drugs.

All these moral arguments are used to suggest that the state cannot allow individuals to be responsible for their own actions with regard to taking recreational drugs and so needs to step in and ban drug use. Of course, the same can, and has, been said about alcohol and tobacco. The buying and selling, and consumption, of alcohol has been criminalized, notably of course in the US during prohibition in the 1930s. But other countries also prohibited or severely restricted access to alcohol, such as Iceland, Finland, Norway, czarist Russia and later the Soviet Union, Canada federally and more stringently in some Canadian provinces. And of course, many Islamic countries also criminalize alcohol consumption – though not some other recreational drugs that are illicit in the West. With regard to the moralistic set of reasons for state paternalist intervention on drug use, alcohol is probably more damaging than marijuana or cannabis.[1]

History of drug policy

Many people are surprised at how short a time drug laws have been in operation. There were no laws governing the growing, buying or selling of drugs in the US, UK or Australia until the 20th century; many were not enacted until the 1970s. Actually, that is not strictly true. In 1619, the Virginia Assembly passed legislation requiring every farmer to grow hemp; and in fact hemp was often used as a form of monetary exchange – much as tobacco and cigarettes are used as currency in jails. Cannabis was widely available throughout the 19th century.

While governments offered moralistic reasons for making drugs illegal, one history of laws governing recreational drug use argues that it is a policy driven by, and facilitating, racial discrimination. Drug use by some ethnic groups was made illicit, although the same drug taken in a different form by the white majority avoided, at first, such regulation. Another argument holds that drug restriction policy was first introduced because of concerns about the effects of drug use on military capability. Today the enforcement of drug policy can be seen as an important cornerstone of US foreign policy.

UK

Drugs in the UK were first regulated by the Pharmacy Act of 1868, followed by the Poisons and Pharmacy Act of 1908. These related to drugs in general. The first limited the selling of drugs to pharmacists, while the second brought in regulations about the labelling of drugs. They had a dramatic effect: the deaths per million people through opium overdose were reduced by one third, and the death rate for children under the age of five nearly halved.

The first controls on specific drugs such as morphine, cocaine and cannabis were introduced during the First World War (as part of the Defence of the Realm Act), largely because the government was concerned about their use by soldiers and their effect on their fighting capacity. (Similarly, the UK introduced much stricter regulations on the buying and selling of alcohol, due to concern about its effects on the war effort.) The Act limited the sale and possession of cocaine to authorized persons. It was followed by the Dangerous Drugs Acts of 1920, 1925 and 1928, which further limited importation, exportation, distribution, sale and use of drugs including opium, cocaine, morphine, heroin and, later, coca leaf and cannabis. However, doctors could still prescribe such drugs for medical purposes, one of which covered those dependent on them. Addicts could get their fix from their doctors.

It was under pressure from the US rather than as a result of any specific increase in drug use – which was rare in the 1960s – that the UK enacted the 1964 Dangerous Drugs Act and Drugs (Prevention of Misuse) Act. The former involved the UK signing up to the United Nations convention designed to control the international drug trade and made cultivation of cannabis a criminal offence, while the latter criminalized amphetamine possession. The 1967 Dangerous Drugs Act required doctors to notify the Home Office about addicted patients, but it was the 1971 Misuse of Drugs Act that introduced the various classes of drugs (A, B, C) and much harsher penalties for trafficking and supply.

In the UK there were six Acts controlling all forms of drugs in 60 years, followed by Acts specifically targeted at recreational drugs (four in the space of seven years), then 16 subsequent Acts controlling and criminalizing drugs in 35 years (although some provisions in the later Acts relaxed regulations, others tightened them or made them more punitive). We can therefore see a significant ratcheting up of paternalistic government control in the area of recreational drugs, based on moralistic justifications, entirely against the tenor of its philosophy of responsibility in virtually all other areas of regulatory policy.

US

The first law prohibiting drug use in the US was in California in 1906, banning the smoking of opium in opium dens. This law was explicitly both moral and racial. The justification was to stop young white women and men from visiting Chinese opium dens. The law made smoking opium illegal, but it did not limit the taking of opium in different forms, such as ingesting with alcohol (as laudanum), which is how white Americans generally chose to take opium. There had been earlier federal laws, the first of which was enacted as early as 1848, governing drugs, but these were concerned more with medicinal usage. They required that drugs be properly labelled and sought to ensure the veracity of claims made about their usefulness.

Federal law on recreational drugs really began with the Harrison Narcotics Act of 1914. This was a regulatory Act that required importers, manufacturers and distributors of cocaine and opium to register with the government, keep records of all transactions and pay tax on those transactions. It was legal for doctors to prescribe these drugs for medical purposes; however, some law enforcement authorities did not consider prescribing to addicts to be legitimate medical use and many medical practitioners were prosecuted for such practices. Hence doctors tended to stop prescribing drugs that came within the ambit of the Harrison Act, driving addicts to black market supplies. The Marihuana [*sic*] Tax Act of 1937 added a $1 'nuisance tax' on the distribution of marijuana. While ostensibly a tax bill, it required that individuals present their goods for a tax stamp. Applying for the stamp could be used to suggest that they had previously been illegally distributing the drug and could lead to prosecution. Several subsequent laws increased the penalties for illegally selling drugs, but no further explicit restrictions were adopted. Most states, however, banned marijuana completely. The Boggs Act of 1951 established mandatory prison sentences for drug offences, and the 1956 Narcotic Control Act further increased penalties, including the death penalty for selling heroin to youths. The 1965 Drug Abuse Control Amendments was designed to mitigate problems with the abuse of depressants, stimulants and hallucinogens, and was directed at prescribers rather than users.

In 1970, the Controlled Substances Act began what President Nixon described in 1971 as the 'war on drugs'. Again, like the UK 50 years earlier, the major concern and driver of drugs enforcement of Nixon and the US government was the effect of drugs on soldiers in Vietnam. Nixon maintained that the abuse of substances was public enemy number one in the US and in 1973 set up the Drug Enforcement Administration (DEA). During the 1980s, drug abuse became a public issue, with new forms of cocaine ('crack') causing media frenzy; by 1989, 27 per cent of the American public thought drug abuse was the most important issue facing the country (up from 6 per cent just four years earlier). Federal drug convictions also rose steeply in the 1980s – from 5,244 in 1980 to 12,285 by 1986 – comprising half the increase of all federal offences in that period. Possession rather than supply was targeted more heavily, and the number convicted of simple possession increased more than fourfold in that period. More federal Acts followed in the 1980s. The Anti-Drug Abuse Acts of 1986 and 1988 turned the rehabilitative drug enforcement system into a punitive one, with minimum mandatory sentences. It also brought synthetically derived drugs within its ambit. US law also allows the temporary scheduling, without further legislative action, of any new drug that appears.

Since the 1990s, more concern has been raised over such synthetic drugs. Methamphetamine first emerged in the 1960s, but was not widely used. It was added as a Schedule II drug in 1970. However, as a drug of choice, it took off in the 1990s; major factories opened in Mexico and border states, making it widely available. Over the past decade, opioid abuse has also become a major issue for the US. Opioids are a set of drugs lawfully prescribed for pain relief, which give a sense of well-being much like morphine. Strongly pushed by pharmaceutical companies which emphasized their pain-killing effects, they have turned out to be highly addictive. They are now widely traded on the black market.

We can see that in the US, too, drug laws have been considerably ratcheted up over time. These drug laws have had a major effect on the prison population. Between 1984 and 1999, the number of defendants charged with a drug offence increased 3 per cent annually, from 11,854 to 29,306. Since 2010, the DEA has been arresting between 30,000 and 40,000 annually, while local law officers arrest between 1.3 and 1.6 million people for drug offences each year, mostly for possession. Not all convicted of such offences receive jail sentences. However, drug offenders now account for more than a quarter of the entire US prison population – around 16 per cent of prisoners in state jails and over half of all federal prisoners are there for drug offences. The incarceration rate in the US, the number of people in jail per 100,000 of the population, is almost 50 per cent higher than in most Western nations. Almost all drug offenders in US prisons have committed non-violent crimes.

The racial nature of drug laws is also demonstrated by the fact that, despite 75 per cent of the US population self-identifying as white, and only 13 per cent as black, and while there is no significant difference between drug use across the racial groups, almost 75 per cent of those in jail for drug offences are black. In other words, if you use drugs, you are 52 times more likely to be given a jail sentence for that usage if you are black rather than white. In 2014, the Obama administration announced a new National Drug Control Strategy, aiming to find alternatives to incarceration. Rates of jailing for drug offences have been reduced, but not yet significantly.

Deaths from drug overdoses passed 70,000 in the US in 2017, up from 37,500 in 2000 and 12,500 in 1980. In part, this is due to illegal drugs being more readily available as distribution networks expand from urban to rural areas, but it is also due to rising addiction rates for prescription pills. Cocaine spiked for overdoses in the early 2000s, and has risen to around three per 100,000 people now; prescription opioids approach four per 100,000; heroin just over four; with synthetic opioids approaching six. Methamphetamine is around two, methadone and other illegal drugs around one per 100,000, and other drugs (usually through suicide) at about three per 100,000. While urban areas have the highest concentration of illegal drug overdoses, rural areas have the highest level for opioids.

We can see, therefore, that drugs are a major social problem in the US. These sorts of figures lead many to believe that the 'war on drugs' has been lost and a new approach is needed. To that end, over the past 30 years several states have started to relax some of their drug laws. Many passed laws to legalize the consumption, possession and sale of marijuana. Medicinal marijuana has been legalized by 48 states, and nine have legalized it for recreational use.

Around 10 per cent of the population admit to having taken some form of illicit drug in the previous month, while around 50 per cent of college students admit having tried illicit drugs. So, despite all the laws, large numbers of people are choosing to take drugs.

Australia

Before Federation in 1901, the original colonies had few laws about recreational drugs, but several of the states, like California, had passed laws against smoking opium largely directed at the Chinese community. While there is a suggestion that in the 1920s Australia had the highest per capita consumption of heroin in the world, its drug laws largely followed international conventions concerned with drug trade. Today, most of the laws governing drugs policies are still enacted at the level of the states. Though prohibiting most of the major recreational drugs, South Australia, the Northern Territory and the ACT have decriminalized cannabis use (civil penalties are applicable under certain criteria). In most Australian states, cannabis possession is not normally penalized; rather, people are sent for education and/or assessment for treatment, though if they fail to attend they may be charged.

The Federal Single Convention on Narcotic Drugs, passed in 1961, updated all international conventions and created a prohibitionist stance on recreational drugs (outside of alcohol and tobacco). (Australia did have some fierce regulatory laws on alcohol that were relaxed from the mid-1970s onwards.) Other federal drug laws include the Narcotic Drugs Act of 1967, covering the medical use of cannabis, and the 1995 Criminal Code, Part 9.1, which covers serious drug offences such as manufacture, importation and supply. By 1970, every state in Australia had laws making drug supply a separate offence from use or possession, replacing the regulatory offences for misusing a medicine.

Australia brought in a new strategy in the 2000s to focus on harm reduction, rather than reduce drug use through punishment and treatment and limit supply through customs and policing. However, only 2 per cent of federal funds related to drugs go into harm reduction, with two thirds spent on law enforcement. There are moves towards viewing drug abuse as a health issue, and drug use as a human rights issue. The head of the federal government's Ice (methamphetamine) taskforce, Ken Lay, suggested 'you can't arrest your way out of the problem' and former Australian Federal Police Commissioner Mick Palmer has stated that 'drug law enforcement has had little impact on the Australian drug market'. Most Australians do not support prison sentences for drug possession (only 5 per cent think it appropriate for cannabis, rising to 24 per cent for heroin). Majority opinion favours decriminalization, though not legalization.

How great a problem is recreational drug use?

Because of the illegality of amphetamines, cocaine and cannabis and illegal use of opioids, it is hard to estimate the precise number of people who take these drugs, how many are problem users and what harms their use causes them, their families and society at large. Most estimates are based on anonymous surveys, estimates of production and assumptions based on drug seizures. Estimates of the number of people who use illicit drugs across the world vary from 149 to 271 million people, estimated at between 125 and 203 million cannabis users; 15–39 million problem users of opioids, amphetamines or cocaine; and 11–21 million injecting drugs, mostly heroin. Certainly, drug use seems highest in rich countries and those close to the source of production, but there is little data on drugs in poorer, low-use countries. Globally, in 2010 it was estimated that the two most common forms of illicit drug dependence are opioids and amphetamines (15.4 million and 17.2 million estimated cases, respectively) followed by cannabis dependency at 13.1 million, with 6.9 million cocaine-dependent persons. Around two thirds of dependent addicts are males. The distribution of drug type varies across regions, with an estimated 58 per cent of amphetamine dependence cases found across Asia (9.3 million cases), but the highest-prevalence estimates were for South East Asia and Australasia. North and Latin America have the highest levels of cocaine dependence, with Australasia having among the highest levels of opioid dependence.

Drug use continues to increase around the world. In the US, it is estimated from surveys that around 25 million people aged 12 or over (almost 10 per cent of the population) had used an illicit drug at least once a month. About 20 million (7.5 per cent of the population) took marijuana in some form, with 6.5 million taking drugs for recreational purposes, both prescription and non-prescription, including stimulants, tranquillizers and hallucinogens (including LSD, ecstasy and other synthetic drugs). Methamphetamine use is also growing, with around 600,000 users. Cocaine and heroin, meanwhile, have seen a slight decline in recent years (about 2–2.5 million people), though the use of both heroin and cocaine tends to fluctuate over time with variations in price and fashions.

In Australia, there have been around 1,500–1,800 overdose deaths per year since 2010. A 2017 report described 1,808 drug-induced deaths in 2016, caused, in order of numbers, by benzodiazepines (such as Valium), legal opioids (such as oxycodones), methamphetamines and heroin. We can see therefore that in Australia, as indeed in the US and UK, legal drugs cause more deaths than illegal ones. Since the beginning of the 21st century, cannabis use among Australians seems to have declined in the younger age group (14 to 39), from 29 per cent in 2001 to 22 per cent in 2016, but has increased slightly in people over 40, meaning the average age of cannabis users has increased from 29 to 34, though the young are still more likely overall to use cannabis. Cannabis is used more frequently than other drugs such as ecstasy and cocaine. Specifically, 36 per cent of people who used cannabis did so as often as once a week or more, compared with only 2 per cent and 3 per cent of ecstasy and cocaine users respectively. Males were more likely than females to use cannabis weekly (41 per cent compared with 29 per cent). Around one in five people aged 12–17 report using cannabis in the past week in 2017, slightly higher than in 2001, and significant differences were found in the proportion of students aged 16–17 using cannabis in the past month and for lifetime users between 2017 (31 per cent and 16 per cent respectively) and 2011 (27 per cent and 13 per cent respectively).

Most people who take illicit drugs start in their teens, usually with cannabis, and drug use is highest among people in their late teens and early twenties. As drug use has become normalized over the past 40 years, though, the numbers of older drug users have increased substantially.

Legalization of recreational drugs?

We must ask, why should recreational drugs not be legalized? Why should governments not treat recreational drugs as they treat gambling? Remember that the arguments for banning or restricting gambling were essentially moral, much as they are for drugs. Gambling was regarded as morally wrong, a sign of vicious not virtuous behaviour, destroying families as people frittered their money away. Similarly, for drugs, James Q. Wilson expressed what many believe: 'drug use is wrong because it is immoral and it is immoral, because it enslaves the mind and destroys the soul', and again, 'Tobacco shortens one's life, cocaine debases it. Nicotine alters one's habits, cocaine alters one's soul'. The first restrictions on recreational drugs were also moral – stopping white people from smoking opium – and now they are justified by the effects that drugs have on people, especially the young. As we saw, though, many of the early laws were enacted because of fears that drugs were affecting front-line soldiers, hence it was a pragmatic policy to support the war effort. So should we legalize all drugs? What would happen?

Most of the arguments are theoretical. Opponents argue that full legalization will make society much worse off. It would flood our communities with dangerous drugs and more people would become addicted, there will be more crime, more social dislocation and a greater number of health problems and deaths. Those who want to go for full legalization suggest that this is not so. They argue that, while more people might use drugs occasionally, most will not become addicted. To be sure, as with the liberalization of gambling laws, there would be social problems, and if more people try drugs, the numbers of those who become addicted might increase. However, full legalization can also be accompanied by greater state action to help addicts and, without the stigma of taking drugs being illicit, they can be more easily found and helped. Furthermore, legalization would not simply be a free-for-all. Legalization can be accompanied by strict regulation, as with medical pharmaceuticals.

After all, the entire argument of this book is about government getting the right kinds of regulation in place in all areas of public policy. Regulation can ensure that drugs are sold by qualified practitioners, chemists and drug stores. The quality and strength of drugs can be strictly monitored. Most people who die of overdoses of recreational drugs do so because the drug they take is adulterated with lethal chemicals or is much stronger than they are used to, causing accidental overdose. So, the biggest effect of regulation and making the manufacture and distribution of recreational drugs a normal commercial proposition is that the quality of the drugs will be assured. Indeed, it would be in the interests of legal manufacturers to ensure quality products in order to avoid litigation. Similarly, it would be in their interests to give advice on safe use of their products. They would certainly carry insurance to mitigate their risks and would be likely to offer some level of customer service.

Legalization would have to ensure that underground sellers are driven off the streets. This would entail the price of legal drugs being held at a level that destroys the profits of black marketeers. The government would also need to maintain high levels of vigilance against underground sellers with both heavy fines and prison sentences. However, the idea is that, in time, the criminal underworld would look away from drugs. If legalization and regulation do shut down the black market, it ought to be easier to deter the young from buying drugs. In many parts of the US, it is easier for children as young as 12 to buy marijuana, cocaine or amphetamines than to purchase alcohol; legalization would be likely to delay the age at which young people start taking drugs, and when they do they would be using safer drugs. Legalization will have beneficial social rather than deleterious effects.

Other effects of legalization would include a massive reduction in criminal convictions. First, those convicted of possession would no longer be criminalized. Second, if legal drugs drive out black market drugs, the crime syndicates that currently operate would have to find other forms of employment. Legalization would also enable taxation. Tax revenues from legal drugs could subsidize the state's efforts to combat illegal drug supplies and pay for social schemes to help addicts, so there would be fiscal benefits too.

Is there any evidence about which side of the argument is correct? There is little empirical evidence – what there is I will discuss below, and most of what I discuss comes from the decriminalization of drugs in Portugal. First, I will consider some of the more careful theoretical accounts and some evidence from the decriminalization of cannabis.

The arguments for and against the legalization of all recreational drugs assume that we are looking at a cost–benefit analysis, where the cost is the cost to society through the drug habits of citizens. Outside of the moral arguments against legalization, the main debate is whether or not legalization will increase or decrease drug use. Those who say that it will increase drug use argue that if drugs are legalized, prices will go down and so demand will go up. More people will consume more drugs, because the price has gone down, no punishments will be meted out for possession and there will be less social stigma. Those who support legalization do so on the grounds that demand will not go up dramatically, because government can tax drugs to control price, but they also argue that legalization will help control the quality of the product (and it is variable quality that causes most deaths) and make it easier to have health campaigns for healthy drug use and to help those who do become addicted. They also argue that it will save the public purse the costs of policing criminalization and, indeed, raise revenue for the government.

The issue of demand and supply is more complicated than it might at first appear. Legalization would probably lead to a fall in drug prices; high prices reflect dealers' risks. How much price affects demand depends upon the elasticity of demand. It is problematic to estimate the elasticity of illegal drugs, but estimates across different types of drugs suggest that elasticity across all drugs is below 1 (with cocaine estimated at −0.3, marijuana at −0.4 to −0.5 and heroin at −0.27). Conventional wisdom suggests that demand for addictive drugs is not so responsive to price. However, this does not seem to be the case for cigarettes and alcohol, where heavy users seem more responsive to price than lighter ones. This suggests that falling prices of drugs will have less effect on those who do not currently consume drugs or only consume a little, but might lead to addicts consuming more. (Though of course, some people who would not try an illicit product might try a legal one.)

Legalization would enable the government to exert some control over demand, through its tax policies. Indeed, government could set tax rates at such a high level that prices would not fall. Conventional wisdom suggests that if that were the case, underground suppliers would not leave the market. However, they would have to sell at below market prices, as there could still be deterrent penalties for buying drugs illegally, and the quality of their products would not be assured. The Chicago economist Gary Becker and his co-authors argue that governments can keep underground producers out of business through judicious use of enforcement and punishment.

There are lessons from the US experience of alcohol prohibition here. Legal producers of alcohol largely went out of business and were replaced by underground producers better able to avoid the authorities. After repeal, the legal producers returned and, in the main, replaced the underground producers who turned to other crimes. We should expect the same sort of response with suppliers of drugs, at least domestically. In countries where many of the drugs are produced, production could, without the carrot and stick of US foreign policy, become legal. This would have advantages not only for the GDP and fiscal welfare of those countries, but would also drive out much of the violent crime. Again, legalization would have big advantages for producing nations. Becker and his colleagues show that taxes have major advantages as a means of reducing quantities available when either demand for or supply of the product being taxed is not very elastic, and especially when both are inelastic. This is the case, they argue, with illegal recreational drugs.

We should also note that the authorities tend to go after the smaller drug dealers, not, as many believe, because the major players corruptly pay off officials (though that is undoubtedly often the case), but because it is cheaper to do so. When demand is inelastic, it is optimal to target the marginal suppliers in enforcing quantity control. However, with excise taxes the opposite is the case: enforcing tax on the major supplies is optimal. As Milton Friedman quipped, the role of the government in recreational drugs has been to create and maintain drug cartels, since the bigger players are targeted less. It is strongly in the interests of illegal suppliers to maintain monopolies in their supply, and this is the major cause of violence between competing cartels.

How much revenue would be raised by taxation? Estimates vary widely, depending on assessments of prices and the level of taxation thought to be optimal. As a guide, the 2014 Initiative 71 that legalized cannabis in Washington, DC went into effect in 2015, and brought in $65 million in tax revenue in its first year. As prices then fell when supply increased, the tax revenue declined. Of course, governments could control price by increasing tax as supply increases. There would be massive savings on the enforcement of prohibition, even allowing for the fact that there would still need to be enforcement of the collection of taxes and stopping illegal supplies. Estimates for the US suggest that government spends approximately $41.3 billion annually on disbursements related to the enforcement of prohibition, around $25.7 billion by local and state governments and $15.6 billion by the federal government.

Legalization does not mean that drugs would not be regulated. New synthetic drugs would need to be examined before being licensed for sale. Would all be drugs be available? Crack cocaine is a particularly nasty drug, but it need not be offered for direct sale. Of course, it is easy to turn powdered cocaine into crack – and we must just accept that that is what some will choose to do – but we can note that the popularity of crack cocaine has dropped. Again, drug manufacturers would be likely to warn against turning their product into crack, in order to protect themselves, but making crack illegal would be against the general policy recommendation of this book. Allow people to make their own choices from a regulated and superior set of alternatives. We might also note that it has been argued that crack cocaine was a result of the war on drugs: it was created to help avoid detection.

Regulation can also help keep drugs away from children; in many areas of both the US and the UK police claim that it is easier for children to access drugs than alcohol. Advertising can be regulated too, and the health dangers flagged as they are now for cigarettes and tobacco. Sales could be through pharmacists and licensed outlets, ensuring quality, and there could even be regulations governing sales to addicts, in much the same way as those controlling the gambling habits of addicted gamblers. Not only would legal drugs be of higher purity, but there would be incentives for manufacturers to make them safer. For example, the major problem with ecstasy is that it raises the consumer's body temperature. In some people the increase is so high that they suffer organ failure. Users drink large quantities of water to counteract this rise in temperature, which can in turn also lead to organ failure. In 2003 it was found that mice lacking a certain protein did not suffer these temperature rises when injected with ecstasy. So legal manufacturers might be able to incorporate an element to deactivate the protein in humans that causes the body to overheat. When drugs are legal, manufacturers have incentives to make them safer, not only through production control, but also through testing and experimentation, just as we see in the legal medical drug market.[2]

Drug use has dangers, at work or when driving for example. However, employers can discipline workers for being drunk and could do the same for those high on drugs. Random roadside drug testing is now common across Australian states and territories, although, unlike alcohol, which is permissible up to a legal threshold, one cannot have *any* trace of illicit drugs in one's system. Following legalization, similar laws could be enacted.

This is a somewhat rosy picture. There is no doubt that drugs do cause personal, family and social dislocation. These are reasons for making drugs illegal. However, most people recognize that the war against drugs has been lost, and in the same way as government has relaxed laws directed at gambling, despite increases in problem gambling, legalizing drugs will enable it to help vulnerable people more. Is there evidence of this? One might look back to times when drugs were legal and drug use was far less prevalent. However, since the world has changed so much, that might not be the best evidence. We can, though, look to evidence from Portugal, which has decriminalized all drug taking. Decriminalization is not the same as legalization, but we might learn some lessons from the Portuguese experience.

Decriminalization in Portugal

Portugal decriminalized the use of all drugs in 2001. Many have studied its impact, with conclusions ranging from a disastrous failure to a resounding success. The most extreme claims largely come from cherry-picking statistics, misusing statistics or not understanding the data that have been examined. There is also a remarkably paternalistic assumption in most of the work: everyone seems to assume that decreased use of drugs makes decriminalization a success. However, the point of non-paternalism is to allow people to make a choice. What matters is not how many people choose to take drugs at some point, but rather (1) how many become addicted – how many would like to stop taking drugs but cannot; (2) what the long-term health effects are; and (3) what the overdose or death rates are. Other considerations are the effects upon the Portuguese economy, and the effects on the public purse of spending on drugs policy.

We must first understand what decriminalization of drugs means in Portugal. It is not the same as legalization. Prior to Portugal's drug law reform, it was illegal to possess, acquire or cultivate drugs for personal use. These offences carried a maximum jail sentence of one year. After decriminalization, such activities were not considered a criminal, but rather a public order or administrative offence. Offenders are referred by the police to Dissuasion of Drug Addiction committees (CDTs) which can sanction offenders with community service, fines and, in some cases, ban offenders from certain places including named bars and clubs. Those seen as dependent upon drugs can also be sent for treatment (and custody is still an option for refusal to abide by these conditions). CDTs initiate around 6,000 administrative processes per year against drug users. Over time, the number of cannabis users given such orders has increased, with those using harder drugs, notably heroin, decreasing from around 33 per cent of offenders to about 14 per cent. The decriminalization process also coincided with efforts to refer those dependent on drugs to healthcare providers.

Most commentators believe that decriminalization has been a success. Before decriminalization, Portugal had a relatively low number of lifetime drug users, with only around 8 per cent of people ever having used illicit drugs (compared with the UK, for example, at 34 per cent). However, a relatively large proportion of these were heroin users, and there was great public concern over the growth in HIV and AIDS among intravenously injecting drug users. Since decriminalization, there has been a small increase in drug use overall in Portugal. Occasional and lifetime use both increased, but no more than in other countries during the same period of time, suggesting that decriminalization is not the cause of that rise, especially given that Portugal started from a low base. Problematic drug use seems to have declined (though only marginally), yet in similar countries such as Spain and Italy it has increased. This suggests that decriminalization did not have deleterious effects, and that if anything it helped.

Furthermore, there were positive effects on the crime rate. The numbers of those arrested for drug offences declined substantially in the years following decriminalization, even though the number of administrative orders remained at 6,000 per year on average. Again, this is an opposite trend to that found in Spain and Italy. Furthermore, in the decade since reform the proportion of drug-related offenders in the prison population – that is, those who committed offences under the influence of drugs and/or to fund drug consumption – has dropped from 44 per cent to 21 per cent. Use of heroin prior to going to prison dropped from 44 to 30 per cent and in prison from 27 to 13 per cent. So, again, decriminalization had good effects on crime over and above merely taking a proportion of the population out of crime by redefinition of their behaviour.

Again, evidence from drug seizures suggests real change in drug consumption in Portugal. While the data spike in some years, with big increases, these seizures are of drugs for which Portugal is a transit country for drugs coming from outside Europe to other countries within Europe. These spikes mask an overall decline over time, which again is not true in Italy or Spain, where seizures have gone up over the same time period.

Decriminalization was followed by a sharp decline in the prices of drugs in Portugal, with the price of heroin falling by almost 40 per cent and ecstasy by 60 per cent. Yet lower prices have not led to an increase in demand; indeed, falling prices seem to have been caused by a combination of an increase in supply and a decrease in demand. Evidence from treatment centres also seems to suggest a reduction in demand, as the age of dependent drug users has increased. In 2000, 23 per cent of clients were aged over 34 on first admission; by 2008, this had increased to 34 per cent. HIV and AIDS cases also dropped by 70 per cent and 80 per cent respectively – attributed to harm-reduction initiatives rather than decriminalization itself.

Portugal provides direct evidence that decriminalization of drugs does not have deleterious effects on dependent drug users, nor indeed seems to encourage drug use. Examination of the scattered empirical evidence on decriminalization of illicit drugs from other places also suggests that removing criminal penalties seems to produce small but positive effects. The most beneficial effect is reducing the burden and cost to the criminal justice system. Removing criminal penalties has little or no impact on the prevalence of drug use, and seems to slightly improve the health risks as users are more willing to seek medical help.

Evidence from the Netherlands suggests that the increase in cannabis consumption there was not caused by depenalization as such, but rather a commercialization process, with the rise of 'coffee shops' openly promoting their wares.

Morality and practicality

The justifications for making recreational drugs illegal are moral ones. As the quote from James Q. Wilson suggests, the mind-altering effects of drugs are thought to attack one's basic humanity, in the sense that they change one's reasoning processes and personality. However, so does alcohol. And, we might note, governments and courts are reluctant to force those with psychological problems to take mind-altering drugs to bring sanity. The other issue is the welfare of individuals, their families and society at large. We saw that Lord Windlesham justified banning drugs when their use threatens society as a viable economic, political or social order. However, drug use has ballooned in the UK since 1971 and the UK has flourished economically if not socially. Moreover, alcohol is estimated to damage the economy in terms of lost production far more than drugs, and to cause more family and social problems. More to the point, legalization would relieve the problems caused by drugs, not add to them. We ought to turn the justification around. Rather than asking should we legalize drugs, we need to ask what possible justification do we have, given all the problems with criminalization, for continuing to make them illegal?

One argument against legalization is that, while the public in the UK, the US and Australia are coming around to the view that cannabis ought to be decriminalized or legalized, there are still large majorities against legalizing hard drugs. To be sure, there are political costs, but this book is not about how public policy works, or why we have the policies we do; it is about the responsibilities government and society bear for the policies they do pursue. Drug policy has failed and politicians need to own up to that fact. If they do so, they might be able to persuade the public that legalization is a good idea.

Some have suggested that in a global economy, and with the internet, it is impossible to control markets, including drugs markets. To be sure, legal drugs can be bought online, avoiding local regulations governing them. For example, Viagra, which is actually a recreational drug – at least one that enables a popular form of recreation – is widely bought on the internet. This is largely because in many countries this recreational drug is treated as a medical one. Making it available over the counter would destroy the global market, largely because Viagra bought through the internet is of variable quality. To be sure, there might be a black internet market for some recreational drugs, but this is still preferable to our current situation.

Final word

All the way through this chapter I have been assuming that the war on drugs has failed due to the socially deleterious effects it has had: the numbers of addicts, the numbers of people locked up for choosing a particular pastime, the crime rate and the massive costs to the public purse. However, some argue that the war on drugs has not failed. It has achieved what US political elites want. It is a racist policy that has ensured large numbers of black citizens go to jail. In many US states felons, even after release, lose their voting rights. Hence drugs policy has enabled the Republican Party to disenfranchise a large section of the population who normally vote for their opponents. Some argue that the war on drugs has been a successful element of US foreign policy, enabling it to pay foreign governments for doing what it wants in the drug field, with knock-on effects in other policy areas, and to ensure that rival countries remain poor and conflict-ridden. It is well known, of course, that, despite all the rhetoric, US agencies, including not only the CIA but also the DEA, run drugs themselves when it is to their advantage. So maybe the drugs war is in fact a rip-roaring success, at least for some elements of the US political elite. I have no particular views on this, though it does make sense of what otherwise is a nonsensical policy.

As in the other policy areas, the situation we have in our countries with regard to drug use – the associated crime and incarceration rates, and health and social problems – result from government policy. All I ask is that governments own up to this.

If they want to defend our current laws, they need to admit that the resultant problems exist because they want to pursue a paternalistic moral stance with regard to drugs and to hell with its consequences.

7

Government Responsibility

Governments blame citizens for their own policies. The modern ideology of individualism and personal responsibility adopted by governments has allowed them to push the idea that their citizens must take responsibility for their own lives and be responsible for their own decisions, and therefore for the consequences of those decisions. That means they can be blamed for ill health, their accommodation and other aspects of their lives. Governments do acknowledge certain limits to that claim. They accept that some health conditions are genetic or due to bad luck, that addiction makes responsible behaviour problematic – but these are limits at the margins. Citizens are responsible for their actions, but can only be held responsible for making reasonable choices from the menu of opportunities they face. Government is the major agent setting that menu. In most areas of life, government is responsible for social outcomes, be they good or bad.

The personal responsibility agenda fits with the idea that government should not be trusted. Government should be minimal, meaning its regulations are light or non-existent. However, that simply means that large corporations and powerful individuals can act irresponsibly with no accountability. We see that with food manufacture, with the arms trade and in the gambling industry. We also see it in the finance and banking industries. In other areas, including housing, individual actions prompted by the financial incentives set up by governments have led to a crisis where the poor have no dwellings to live in at all, and the young middle class cannot afford to buy homes as their parents and grandparents did. Government is to blame. I will first review my arguments in the areas I have examined and then look at a set of criticisms that might be levelled at my argument.

Review

I have looked at some policy areas where we might think that government regulatory policies are problematic: gun control, obesity, housing, gambling and drugs. We might also have considered myriad others – transport, the environment, sports policy, gender discrimination in the workplace – or the big one that may make all the rest seem trivial: climate change. The topics I have chosen to discuss were picked for two reasons. First, they are all relatively small or enclosed policy areas where the regulatory issues are comparatively self-contained. Second, I selected these particular ones in order to illustrate different aspects of my argument.

I chose gun control as the first of the policy chapters, since it provides the clearest evidence of how regulations affect behaviour. An important aspect of my argument is that humans, like all animals, respond to incentives. The regulatory framework set by government, no matter how those regulations are framed, sets up an incentive structure for citizens. To that extent, how people act in society is at least partly within the government's control. Whatever outcomes come about, therefore, government must take responsibility. Government cannot simply look at what people do and say 'that is in their control, they are responsible'. The general welfare of society is the government's responsibility.

The regulations governing the buying, selling and use of different forms of firearms vary a great deal from country to country. Among the three countries I have been using as my main case studies, the US stands out on this issue. Indeed, it stands out in the developed world for its relaxed attitude to gun control. It is also a massive outlier when it comes to injuries and deaths from firearms. As we saw in Chapter 2, in all categories – accidents, suicide, homicide, mass murder – the death rate from firearms is much higher in the US than in other countries. While we can observe some compensatory behaviour, particularly in the category of suicide – if someone is determined to kill themselves and firearms are not available, then they will use something else

– this compensatory behaviour does not make up for the ease of using firearms.

Gun control is also a vibrant and controversial political issue in the US because of the passion around the right to bear arms. For those outside the US it is often hard to understand why gun control is so fraught an issue. Given the massive death rate relative to comparable countries, why is introducing stricter regulation controversial? Imagine similar comparisons of death rates for, say, airline safety, workplace safety or childbirth; can we envisage equally intense resistance to regulatory reform?

The US is home to a strong pro-gun lobby group, the NRA, which funds politicians and campaigns against those wanting stricter rules. But it could not be so successful were there not also reasons that many people think justify the freedom to buy guns with so few restrictions. Those reasons are provided in the Second Amendment to the US Constitution, which gives the right to bear arms, and was originally designed to afford people – or, rather, 'the people' – the ability to fight the tyranny of government. The American republic was forged in the crucible of a revolution throwing off the yoke of British rule and demanding the right to self-government. The right to bear arms, following the revolutionary war, seemed a desirable welfare policy. Ever since, the desire that government should regulate this area with a light touch has been a major force in US thought. While most people around the world are aghast at the ease with which people in the US can buy multiple automatic and semi-automatic weapons, let alone other forms of firearms, especially given the high death rate, and many who live in the US would like to see much stronger gun control regulations, for some people the Second Amendment gives an inviolable right to own guns. The issue for them is one of liberty and keeping the paternalistic state off their case.

I then turned to the issue of body shape and the obesity crisis. The growing numbers of people who are overweight, obese, indeed morbidly obese, in the developed world has increased rapidly over the past three decades. Body shape itself has changed over the years. It is well known that diet has an effect on body shape; indeed studies show that people of different cultures tend to be of a shape and height that correlate with their culturally specific diets. Body shape can also signal one's social class – while now the rich tend to be slimmer than poorer people, in the past being large was a demonstration that one ate well. It was a signal of wealth. As society has become wealthier, the size of food portions has also grown. One study not only gives evidence that portion sizes have grown over the past 30 years, but also uses paintings of the Last Supper, a standard subject in Christian culture, to show that portion sizes as depicted in these paintings have increased over time, almost certainly reflecting contemporary expectations of portion size at such meals. However, the science of nutrition has demonstrated that while portion size is something to be concerned about, a major contributing factor to obesity is the excessive intake of sugar and, to a lesser extent, fatty products and salt. As reported in Chapter 3, sweetened carbonated drinks have an enormous effect on body shape; even those which use sweeteners that do not have a (known) direct effect on body shape engender a sweeter tooth in their consumers, making other sweet products more appealing to them.

Governments could limit the amount of sugars, refined carbohydrates and salts in manufactured food either directly or through taxes, or a combination of both. They could also regulate their use in restaurants and cafes. Consumers could still eat the same amounts of food and drink the same quantity of liquids and yet not put on as much weight as they currently do. This is an area where food manufacture and preparation have changed, but government regulation has not kept pace. Food manufacturers, through experiment and theoretical enquiry, have discovered how to create foodstuffs that appeal to people, especially the young. People have a natural, evolutionarily developed desire for sweetness, fats and salt. These tastes once served us well; now our intake is excessive, yet their attraction remains. Manufacturers have also artificially created flavours that have great appeal to our taste buds, to such an extent that they can trigger cravings. In both cases, manufacturers are manipulating humans' evolved responses in order to incentivize behaviour which, in this case, is not to human advantage. Furthermore, while food manufacturers once manipulated us without being fully aware of the science, now they understand it well. Governments, despite the wealth of scientific evidence, have not kept up with food manufacturers. This policy area shows how governments have failed to keep track of how their citizens are being manipulated and have failed to counteract that manipulation.

The third policy chapter considers the housing crisis. This is a different type of failure from those discussed in Chapters 2 and 3, for here the crisis has been caused not by government failing to reregulate in response to changing technical and economic conditions, but rather by government itself engineering those conditions. Government, through its policies, has created the housing crisis as it now exists. In the post-war period, especially in the UK (and other European countries) where there was massive bomb damage, there was a felt need for the government to facilitate house building and to take direct action itself on building new dwellings to house a homeless population. In the US and Australia, government became directly involved in house building for slightly different reasons. In the US, the 1930s depression caused major social dislocation which, along with a growing economy after the war, caused large-scale geographical mobility and created a need for new housing. At this time, rural areas lost population and cities grew at an ever-expanding rate. Australia faced a fast-growing population due to immigration, which fed economic growth through new industry, and these workers had to be housed. Evidence was growing, too, that poor housing conditions were a major health concern. These factors led governments to directly finance public housing. They also facilitated private developments for both home ownership and rented accommodation. In many places they used rent control to ensure accommodation remained affordable, and enforced regulations governing the quality of accommodation.

From the 1970s onwards, governments changed course and adopted, largely independently of each other, a two-pronged strategy that created the current housing crisis. First, they started to get out of the business of providing good-quality public housing at affordable rents. They ended or reduced their direct state-funded building programmes, expecting the private and non-profit sectors to fill the gap. They ended rent control in order to encourage the private sector to provide rental accommodation, thereby pushing up the costs of private renting and increasing pressures on public and not-for-profit housing at precisely the same time that the number of rentable units in these areas was decreasing. Second, they created tax incentives for people to buy their own properties. In the UK, this policy of the right-to-buy public housing at bargain prices denuded public sector housing. Of course, the policy was very popular because those in public (council) accommodation who could afford to buy did so, and then often sold quickly in order to move up the property ladder. This helped fuel a massive increase in property prices that could not be sustained when the economy dipped. Some families who had purchased their council homes were stuck with houses worth less than their mortgages; in some cases they lost their homes and required rehousing in the now attenuated stock of housing left in public hands. While the right-to-buy policy was popular among those in public housing, it actually removed a vast tranche of housing (and public wealth) out of the public sector. There were simply not the funds, nor often the will, to replace it with new builds.

The second government policy prong that created the housing crisis was fiscal. Governments provided tax incentives to buy property. Again, this policy proved popular with citizens, enabling them to buy homes for themselves. It fits with the idea of personal freedom to create one's dwelling to one's personal taste and materially instantiates rights in a property-owning society. However, these tax incentives go well beyond the right of a household or a person to buy a home to live in. It also gives incentives to those who are wealthy enough to buy second, third or as many properties as the state can afford to subsidize. These include second or 'holiday' homes or 'pieds-à-terre' near one's work. The fiscal regime also encourages people to buy properties to rent. Since they are private individuals and not developers, buying property to rent out does little to encourage new builds. Private individuals tend to want to purchase older properties, and to buy from other private individuals rather than from developers with new-build properties. The resulting pressure on existing housing stock fuels the property market, and ever-increasing prices and the tax incentives available mean that property is a good investment even if it remains vacant without tenants. This problem is particularly severe in Australia. In Sydney, for example, it is estimated that there are up to a million unoccupied dwellings, despite cripplingly high rents and large numbers of homeless people. This is a complete failure of government policy.

The fourth policy chapter looks at gambling. Here again, governments have altered the law. Relaxing regulations has had a deleterious effect on the amount and degree of problem gambling in society. The case for relaxing gambling regulations is the liberal one that such regulations enforce morality on the population, indeed a specifically Protestant Christian morality upon an increasingly secular population. For the vast majority of people, the liberalization of gambling laws does not cause any problems, but rather opens up freedom – the freedom to legally gamble. Most people do not gamble, or only gamble occasionally for small amounts of money. Others gamble more often and for larger proportions of their income or wealth, but given the pleasure that gambling can bring this is a lifestyle choice that is no worse than spending your money on sporting or musical events, building up collections, and so on. For a few, perhaps 1 in 20 people, gambling becomes a major problem that ruins their lives and those of their immediate family.

Moreover, problem gambling is a medical problem for which one cannot straightforwardly assign personal responsibility. The neurological basis of gambling addiction is now well attested. While the precise neurological mechanisms are not fully understood, we now know that with gambling addiction the brain's reward and pleasure centres become overwhelmed in a feedback loop that leads people to pathologically gamble for short-term reward. It does not provide long-term reward: quite the opposite.

Gambling is also an area, like food manufacture, where government has failed to keep up with the technical innovations, scientific expertise and marketing nous of the industry. Modern gambling machines are specifically designed to maximize how often and how much people will gamble. We might argue that, in a competitive capitalist market, there is nothing wrong with that. Firms are supposed to maximize their profits, and in doing so they create the conditions for consumers to maximize their enjoyment from the products the firms supply. However, these machines exploit the fact that, biologically, our brains have developed to provide rewards in the form of 'highs' for some types of behaviour, for evolutionary advantage.

In some people, neurological bugs (analogous to computer bugs in software – instructions designed for one purpose that cause subsequently installed programs to crash) can lead to the reward system going haywire. When that happens, the welfare benefits of the competitive market are compromised. Rather than maximizing pleasure, gambling addicts may suffer massive financial loss, family break-up and, often, severe depression. Gambling addiction frequently goes together with other addictive and pathological behaviours. We can see, though, that the gambling industry readily exploits problem gamblers. In some ways this is a similar story to what we saw with the obesity crisis. Technical innovations in both the design and manufacture of EGMs and the advent of internet gambling have created a need for careful regulation. Government has started to regulate and work with the industry to deal with these problems; nevertheless, whatever the level of problem gambling in any society, the government must take responsibility, due to its regulatory powers.

The final policy area I discuss is recreational drugs. Recreational drug use is a policy area much like gambling. Here, however, government policy has gone in precisely the opposite direction. Over time, government has increasingly intervened to criminalize recreational drugs – with the exception of alcohol, which instead has seen a relaxation of the regulations governing its production and sale. We have to question why, when government accepts that it is not its role to enforce morality on gambling, it does so with recreational drugs.

There might be some arguments for this policy. Misusing recreational drugs causes severe illness and death, and over time addiction can bring about both minor and major psychological problems. However, legalizing and regulating drug manufacture while taxing supply might well enable government to control drug use far more effectively and help to reduce the death rate. A large proportion of fatalities from recreational drug use derives from inconsistencies in quality, both in terms of strength and of impurities introduced during their manufacture. Legalizing drug production would enable quality control to make recreational drugs safer and give drug users more predictable highs. It could also ensure that the impurities which are particularly associated with fatalities could be excluded. Legalizing drugs would make it easier for people to seek medical attention if they became ill, especially if they started suffering psychological problems. Drug users often hide their addiction from medical practitioners, making diagnosis more difficult.

There are other reasons for restricting drug use: they have deleterious effects on behaviour that can affect people when driving, at the workplace and in other arenas where they might pose a danger to themselves and others. However, legalization could be accompanied by other regulations governing their use. Even now, most police forces have the equipment to test drivers for a variety of drugs beyond alcohol, and employers could be given rights to test workers for drug use where it can be shown that such usage impairs their ability to do the job for which they are paid, or endangers fellow workers.

In all cases these are government regulatory failures.

Criticisms of the argument

Here I consider six potential criticisms of the argument:

- *Evidence.* Policy is more difficult that I claim. I assert that we know that governments could regulate better in the areas I discuss, but is this true? Indeed, some problems may not have solutions because views on what a solution should be differ. Sometimes providing solutions simply changes the nature of the problem. The criticism is that I ignore disagreements over consequences, as well as downplaying the problems of implementation.
- *Government failure.* I have argued that governments are failing in various policy areas. This shows a contradiction in my account. We cannot trust governments to get it right, so rather than saying governments should do more they should do less.
- *Freedom and autonomy.* The responsibility agenda is part of our belief that people ought to be free to make their own choices, and governments should not interfere with individual

autonomy. I put my faith in the nanny state, but ignore the dangers to human autonomy and freedom.

- *Regulation or nudge?* Over the past decade or so the 'nudge agenda' has arisen – it claims to be a form of libertarian paternalism where government can help its citizens choose better options without impinging on liberties and autonomy. Nudge is preferable to regulation.
- *Governments do not fail as badly as I portray.* Governments are not failing as badly as I suggest and their policies are more successful than I admit.
- *Social responsibility.* I have placed the burden of responsibility on governments, but in democracies governments reflect their citizens. The failures I examine are societal failures, not governmental ones. Responsibility ultimately does rest with people and not their governments.

Having examined and answered these objections, I will see how far my argument can be directed more broadly than the five constrained issues that I consider in the policy chapters.

Evidence and feasibility

My main purpose is to place responsibility for social outcomes on government. The amount of gun crime, the degree and distribution of obesity, the degree and distribution of homelessness, gambling addiction and the crime and incarceration rate for recreational drugs are all due to government-set incentives. I have made it obvious that I think governments, at least in some countries, are failing their citizens in these policy areas because the evidence is clear. However, it might be claimed that I am too harsh on government. I have suggested that we know how government policy has affected these social outcomes; some might argue that I am giving far too much credit to science and social science.

There are two general lines of argument that might suggest that these areas do not demonstrate policy failure, or at least do not necessarily show policy failure in the obvious manner I suggest. The first line of argument is that I have helped myself to assumptions about what the best consequences are. I will deal with that swiftly. To be sure, I have assumed that fewer deaths from guns is better than more; that obesity and homelessness are genuine problems; and that gambling and recreational drug use are not in themselves a problem, but the consequences that follow are and need to be addressed by government. If anyone disagrees, then all I ask is that they are explicit in that disagreement, and defend current policies. These people need to take responsibility for their case, and give reasons why these consequences are acceptable, and not blame others for them.

The second general argument takes two forms. First the evidence is not as clear-cut as I claim. Second, some areas are 'wicked problems' that have no solution.

Evidence

Is the evidence clear? Should governments base their solutions on scientific evidence? There are many political reasons why government does not follow the advice of experts. Scientists do not always present their evidence in a policy-oriented manner. On any issue there is always some debate and disagreement which can be exploited by contrary forces. One of the major problems is that research and writing in science and public policy are two different things. Scientists are sceptical; they are always questioning current beliefs and evidence. They constantly seek new evidence and new results, even if those results are only marginally different from previous ones. As philosophers of science continually point out, nothing discovered in science is certain. We have degrees of belief in our findings: some results we strongly believe, others we believe but are less sure are correct. Scientists, in order to maintain their reputations, tend to hedge their bets a little, and not to overstate their findings – at least in the scientific literature; university public relations departments increasingly issue press releases that make grander claims, and scientists themselves are under pressure to do so in blogs and tweets. All too often, when they give policy advice, scientists act like scientists. When doing public policy, one still needs to be critical, but not of one's policy prescriptions. Here one needs to be an advocate.

I chose the topics I did because I think the evidence is clear, and I have tried to present an overview of that evidence in the five policy chapters. There can be little doubt that the US's lax gun control laws are the cause of its massive firearms death rate in comparison to other developed countries. It is true that in the literature one can find academic articles that dispute aspects of the gun control argument.

So, for example, Jeanine Baker and Samara McPhedran question whether the tightened National Firearms Agreement (NFA) legislation and gun buyback in Australia following the Port Arthur massacre had any real effect on homicides or the suicide rate. They use the autoregressive integrated moving average (ARIMA) method to predict sudden deaths in different categories based on previous trends prior to that legislation. ARIMA estimates future values of deaths over time by a linear combination of past values, and errors estimated from past values, using a maximum likelihood fit. Bounds are set at the 95 per cent confidence interval and future values (after 1996) are estimated. Then the real values are plugged into the model.

Baker and McPhedran found that the actual homicide rate falls within the bounds of the 95 per cent confidence interval that was estimated for the dates after the change in legislation. In other words, the actual rate of murders was within estimates made assuming away the legislation. They conclude that we cannot trust that the legislation had any effect on the murder rate. Accidental deaths and suicides, both by firearms and by other means, do fall below the 95 per cent interval from the estimated values. One might think Baker and McPhedran ought to conclude therefore that this shows that the legislation did reduce death rates in these areas. However, they caution that we cannot make that inference. They say that the number of accidental deaths is small with substantial variation, so we cannot trust the seeming fall. Meanwhile, they note that the overall suicide rate increased immediately after the NFA and conclude therefore that suicide rates in Australia were influenced by other social changes, such as suicide prevention programmes.

Baker and McPhedran's article is a careful and properly critical academic analysis. They do not state, for example, that we cannot conclude that the NFA did not reduce the murder, accidental death or suicide rate, even though it meant there are far fewer firearms in Australia, just that we cannot conclude that it did. We might say, but why should we think that it did not? Well, for example, the bulk of murderers who use guns are criminals or terrorists who could gain access to illegal weapons no matter what the law. And if someone is determined to kill themselves, then they will find other means if guns are not available. But fewer guns will surely mean fewer accidents, even if pre-1996 legislation in Australia was sufficiently tight that many types of accident which occur in the US, such as children coming across guns and killing family members, could not have happened. The problem for evidence-based policy and for science is that pinning down causation – 'causal inference' in the statistician's lingo – from evidence is difficult.

Any set of observational data, such as data on homicide, suicide or accident rates, that we try to explain by some particular factor – such as new legislation – can always be criticized on the ground that there *might be* confounding factors. Confounding factors essentially mean other things going on that are not in the statistical model, such as, in the Baker and McPhedran article, other social forces. And, of course, the suicide rate will be affected by other factors, which might indeed explain its increase immediately after the NFA. However, that does not mean that we should ignore the fact that, post-1996, the overall trend in suicides declined more steeply than its ARIMA prediction. We can be unduly sceptical about discoveries, especially in areas of great concern. After all, we need to consider other background knowledge. We know people respond to incentives and easier access to the means of suicide will surely increase the suicide rate for any given set of potential perpetrators given any level of determination to kill themselves. Similarly for the homicide and accident rates. Rather than using some fancy statistics to suggest that changes in legislation might not have the effects that the descriptive statistics indicate, we should try to identify factors other than the legislation that explain the effects. Of course, any other claim might be disputed on the ground that the observational data might be wrong due to other confounding factors not yet thought of.

Baker and McPhedran's article only considers a specific piece of gun legislation in Australia, and the demonstrated behavioural effects of that one piece of legislation. It cannot be used to dispute the wide variety of evidence about the effects of firearm legislation on death rates around the world. However, the way of academia is that every piece of evidence is open to such potential problems. Herein lies the problem that science has with affecting policy. Alternative voices can often be heard on any issue. Government needs to listen to what the majority of voices say. We cannot ignore the majority voice on the grounds that science by nature is sceptical – or if we do, we have to take responsibility for that refusal to act. We see that government does not act responsibly in that way. The refusal of governments to listen to the overwhelming scientific evidence on global climate change is a stark and terrifying testament to that fact.

We can find similarly contrary evidence on the problem of obesity. Here the issue of evidence is slightly different. Few, if any, medical experts dispute the fact that the obesity crisis is at least partly caused by the nature of modern food manufacture. Few doubt that saturated fats, salts and sugars in food, and sugars in carbonated drinks, play an important role in that process. Disagreement lies in how big a role the medical experts think they play. Again, other confounding factors exist: portion size and how much exercise people take these days in comparison to the past, for example. However, while we can acknowledge that such 'confounding factors' affect body shape, we should not refuse to take action on regulating food manufacture on the grounds that science has not reached unanimity over the precise amount of difference that additives make in the food-manufacturing process. Indeed, one scientific response would be to make the regulatory changes so science can gather data to help us better answer that question. We should not allow politicians off the hook of their responsibilities for social outcomes with the excuse that the science has not reached unanimous agreement, or that there is a scientific article here or there that challenges some of the findings of other scientific articles. There is agreement that these additives affect body shape. Government should act on that agreement, and not on other more minor disagreements that concern the degree of the effect.

As we proceed to housing, gambling and drugs, we find the issues become more complex. Gambling is less so in many ways, though as we saw in Chapter 5 the science there is potentially compromised by its funding sources. Industry funding seems to make academics especially sceptical of some of their own findings. For example, Nicki Dowling and colleagues discuss EGMs. After reviewing a lot of evidence that shows how EGMs seem to foster pathological gambling more than other forms of gambling (as I report in Chapter 5), they go on to say that those conclusions are not supported by the evidence. Why this seemingly perverse conclusion? They say it is because the evidence 'has yet to establish the absolute "addictive" potential of EGMs relative to other forms of gambling'. Yet the correlations are there; we just do not have the instruments for the precision they seem to require. They do go on to say that 'the association between EGMs and problem gambling cannot be discounted. It is therefore appropriate for research to attempt to evaluate the impact of modifying machine characteristics on problem gambling behaviour.' The problem with that sort of academic writing is that it seems simply to be a self-interested request for more money so the researchers can do more research in order to reach more definite conclusions. We can always do more research, but government should act on the best results we have so far.

Because there are always contrary views, I have tried to make use of systematic review and meta-analysis which together provide the strongest evidence of the current empirical wisdom of those that analyze these areas. Empirical evidence is important, not just 'expert opinion'. Government should make greater use of systematic review and meta-analysis, perhaps even commissioning it, but only using such analyses once they have been published in one of the best relevant peer-reviewed journals. Governments shouldn't cherry-pick from articles, or cherry-pick specific findings from research, ignoring other results. They should use the bulk of evidence. Systematic review and meta-analysis is where to find that. The important point to note, however, is that we should never use disagreement as a reason for doing nothing.

I ought to mention in passing the derogation of experts we have seen in the UK Brexit Leave campaign, and the total disregard of evidence we see from Trump and his supporters, climate change deniers and the like. I ignore that nonsense in this book. I assume any one who reads this kind of book does not require my denunciation of the wilful disregard of evidence for private or political purposes.

Wicked problems

The idea of 'wicked problems' arose in the 1970s, but has become more popular among policy scientists in the past decade or so. Today the term is used in numerous different ways. In its original incarnation (in a 1973 article by Rittel and Webber), the basic idea was that any solution to a problem changes our understanding of that problem. Once that new understanding is created, the – or at least a – problem remains. Rittel and Webber also suggested that one cannot understand problems without providing solutions, for there is no definitive statement of what the problem is until one has thought of potential solutions. Wicked problems have no stopping rule, they say, since there are no definitive answers and those that are given are neither right nor wrong, just better or worse or 'good enough'. Each problem is unique, and we need to keep changing policy to keep up with the changing nature of the issue, as the previous 'solutions' redefine it. Finally, Rittel and Webber suggest that problems might have multiple different and competing solutions. Today, wicked problems are sometimes presented through the lens of complexity. Social life is so complex that we cannot really grapple with solutions, merely with trying to make life easier.

For a concrete example of all this, think back to the chapter on housing policy, where one of the issues I raised was rent control. Rent and quality controls of accommodation are disliked by economists since they impede market solutions. If one person is prepared to pay more for an item than other people, why should not the seller sell to the highest bidder? If rents are kept low, then property owners have little incentive to improve their properties. Keeping rents low will also affect the relative value of housing and discourage investment in new properties, and so on. The problem I alluded to was the removal of rent control at the same time as government was both reducing the amount of housing that it was building and encouraging wealthier people to buy additional properties. The idea was that removing rent control would encourage new builds; so, while overall rents would rise, they would meet a natural cap as new properties were created to fulfil demand. However, the tax incentives, together with what appears to be the never-ending inflation of house values, mean that for many it is not worthwhile renting at prices that people who are homeless can afford, a situation recently exacerbated by the rise of Airbnb.

Removing rent controls certainly eased problems with the market that existed in many parts of the world in the 1970s. Properties that owners had felt were not worth renting out were released on to the market and, arguably, more was spent improving properties once rent controls were lifted. The policy did help to encourage developers to produce more private new-build properties, but not enough to fill the gap left by the government abandoning its role in housing. It also solved various implementation problems. In some regulatory systems, rents were controlled for long-term tenants, who simply rerented to others, making money out of property that was not theirs. Therein lies a problem. 'Rent control' is an idea not a policy. The precise details of how one goes about controlling rents is a policy. In the UK, rent control was relatively light-handed. Both tenant and landlord could ask for the rent to be reviewed by the local council and rents could go up or down according to national guidelines. In many cities in the US, however, where rent control still exists, regulations are often much tighter, designed to make it difficult for landlords to increase rents for sitting tenants, making 'secondary renting' a problem.

The UK light-touch version, where either party can request a review on a regular basis, is a preferable model. However, the issue I am pointing up is not so much canvassing its reintroduction, but rather how removing it helped create the problems we now have, as it came in conjunction with other policies. Another way of overcoming the empty property problem would be to restore old laws governing the rights of squatters. Again, the UK from the 1960s onwards, at the same time as all the other changes in housing law, saw the removal of common law provisions that had given people rights to occupy unused and derelict buildings. These rights provided strong reasons for property owners not to allow their properties to remain empty for long periods or to become derelict, but to rent them out; this policy would bring rents down without having to resort to rent control. Of course, in the 1960s, large-scale developers would sometimes completely trash buildings to render them uninhabitable and discourage squatting. This could be countered by laws taking into public ownership buildings that are unused or derelict for, say, one year and a day, which might lead to a more efficient use of property.

So we can see how solutions can lead to new problems, then new solutions to further difficulties. And we can call this cycle a 'wicked problem'. It seems a nice phrase. Rittel and Webber claim that wicked problems cannot be solved and must be tackled using political rather than scientific judgements. If it is argued, as it sometimes is, that it therefore follows that we should not bother taking in scientific evidence or listening to experts, then the claim is dubious at best. It is certainly the case that any policy may not work as originally intended. Any policy can have unintended side effects that might need later amelioration. Any policy might satisfy some people and not others. Any policy can be gamed, so that even if it works for a while, over time it becomes less effective. But any policy can also be amended and changed to deal with these sorts of shifting circumstances. The notion that a problem is wicked because it is not susceptible to easy solutions that satisfy everyone simultaneously is likely to apply to each and every policy issue. The idea that therefore we should not act in such cases is an excuse for never doing anything. Cyclical policies that shift problems around would often be a better policy device than doing nothing at all. Furthermore, we should not simply privilege the status quo. The status quo always advantages some, but those beneficiaries should not be privileged.

Problems can sometimes be broken down into component parts and solved piecemeal. Sometimes more radical change is desirable. However, government cannot avoid its responsibility for how society runs on the grounds that the issues are problematic, the solutions difficult or that the problem is 'wicked'. Agents are as responsible for an outcome if they do nothing as if they do something. In the famous trolley dilemma, you must decide whether or not to pull the lever to switch the trolley (or tram) on to another track where it will kill one person but five will be saved. If you pull the lever you are responsible for killing the one person. Doing nothing does not absolve you of responsibility for letting the five people die. Government decisions are like that all the time. Most policies will damage the interests of some people and help those of others. Whether the government pulls the lever or not, whether it acts or not, it bears responsibility for the outcomes, even if the problem has the characteristics of being wicked.

The main problem with the whole idea that there are wicked problems is that the concept itself can be strategically gamed. One aspect of a wicked problem is that there is disagreement over the desirable properties of the issue, and dispute or controversy over the right ways to go about dealing with it. However, that cannot be a defining feature, since any government policy will attract disagreement over the desirable properties of the outcome, for any rule or regulation entails winners and losers. And, anyway, it is up to government to *decide* what it thinks is desirable and to take responsibility for that decision. If we then say that there is controversy over the right way of dealing with the problem, then it can be gamed. All it takes to make controversy is for someone to loudly and persistently claim that they disagree with others. Controversies are continually created by shock jocks and the media, by finding some social media rant by someone somewhere and proclaiming the issue is controversial. Claiming that wicked problems are ones where there is disagreement over what is desirable makes it possible to say all problems are wicked. Describing a problem as wicked adds nothing to simply saying it is a problem. And it is the job of government to try to deal with problems and difficulties. Joshua Newman and Brian Head class gun violence as a wicked 'unsolvable problem' in the US, but one readily solvable in other countries. Quite!

Government failure

The argument I have been pressing is contradictory. I show that governments have poor policies in some areas and say we need them to do more in those areas. But if they always get things wrong, then we cannot trust them to get the regulations right. We should not ask government to regulate more, we should ask them to do less.

This objection is partly theoretical and partly empirical. The theoretical objection, often associated with the economic or 'public choice' approach to the study of government, says that I am assuming that governments are benevolent and want to produce welfare-enhancing policies, but in fact they are filled with self-interested actors who are trying to maximize their own welfare, and will only maximize that of society if the correct incentives are in place for them to do so. In most fields there is 'regulatory capture', so government regulations basically exist for the benefit of the industry or for government officials themselves. Indeed, we might find evidence of that claim in my case studies. I suggested at the end of Chapter 6 that maybe the drug war is not a failure, but in fact is a US foreign and domestic policy success, helping the US dominate its neighbours and enable white elites to keep the black population under their thumb. Less cynically, it provides employment for agents in the DEA and other law enforcement agencies and a steady supply of cheap labour for the private prison service, and gives elected politicians a nice justification for high crime rates that they can then pontificate about and spend money on. And, of course, it might be so dirty that the drug barons pay off politicians not to legalize drugs which might threaten their criminal empires. Light regulation is in the interests of food manufacturers and fast food stores which are big money spinners; US politicians are in the pockets of the NRA which spends vast amounts of money financing election campaigns and political adverts designed to keep the American public ignorant and pretend issues of gun regulation are really about 'taking your guns away'. Similarly, gambling laws were relaxed and self-regulation promoted because that is in the interests of the gambling industry, and, as I described, it funds most of the research into its effects.

At the detailed policy-generation level, we would tell different stories with different elements for each issue area and within each country. However, the general outline across all countries will be similar. The political or policy science answer is that government is subject to pressures from rent-seeking industry that wants light regulation of some aspects, so it can maximize its profits, and heavier regulation of others, in order to keep out competition. Firms press not for the regulations that are best for consumers, but for those that are best for themselves.

When making decisions, government needs information; and while it can source information from scientists and concerned lobby groups as well as voters themselves, it is industry that provides the easiest and cheapest source of information. After all, the industry itself has inside knowledge, and given that its interests are concentrated and those of the public diffused, it is in industry's own interest to fund research. Hence the science can become biased. The industry might seek to hide or downplay results it does not like, while promoting favourable results. At a still earlier stage, it can simply direct independent researchers into the sorts of questions that suit the industry rather than the consumer. Sometimes, when problems become too obvious, as became the case with gambling addiction, it is in the industry's own interest to conduct research into the problem and come up with solutions. But we cannot assume that the findings thus derived will be optimal for consumers. Industry might prefer sticking plaster solutions rather than preventing the injury in the first place.

So, giving a political science answer to why government provides suboptimal solutions is relatively easy. It is a collective action problem. Industry is concentrated and has intense interests in certain regulations; consumers are a larger group with broader and more diffuse interests. Hence both information provided to government and that to the public at large is biased towards industry. Second, the industry has relatively more to spend and so it can fund political parties and candidates. We can see this most clearly with the gun lobby in the US. The NRA, while nominally an organization for gun users, is largely funded by gun manufacturers and dealers. It provides political backing to US politicians and can use its massive resources to directly campaign against candidates who lobby for gun regulations that it does not approve of. What we see explicitly for the gun lobby in the US is also the case, often more subtly and covertly, for other industries, such as the gambling industry, notably in Australia, and for the pharmaceutical industry all over the world.

The housing crisis is rather different. Here government pandered to the interests of a specific set of voters – ones, moreover, whose support could be shifted from one party to another. The right-to-buy policy in the UK, for example, appealed to Labour-supporting council house renters, encouraging them to shift their support to the rival Conservative Party which introduced it. Once they were home owners, they became more interested in interest rate policy, an economic issue that is more 'owned' by the Conservative than the Labour Party (that is, the electorate tends to trust the Conservatives more than Labour in this policy area).

We can, then, explain bad policies by informational, monetary and electorally induced incentives for parties and politicians. However, this book is not designed to give political science answers to why we have the policies that are in place around the world. Rather, it is intended as a book of social and political philosophy, albeit one that has a firmer grip upon policy issues than most. We can explain how government generates its policies through these political and electorally induced incentives. My focus here, however, is on how these policies are defended by government by reasons which are underpinned by a philosophy of personal responsibility. And that philosophy is as much a part of left-wing as right-wing thinking. I want to investigate the reasons given for these moves, and suggest that their philosophical justification is wanting.

I do not consider these factors to be criticisms of the argument. We can explain why governments do not use evidence-based policy as often as they should. Governments are ideological. They pander to their core voters. They kowtow to their paymasters. They fear backlash from powerful industries, media interests and lobby groups. Governments do not always understand policy advice, and worry about making changes that might affect their short-term popularity, because politicians are famously myopic.

Lawyers tend to dominate legislatures and parliaments, and lawyers are trained to argue a case from either side.

However, this is not a political science or public policy book designed to explain policy failure. It is one of normative political philosophy. I leave the empirical reasons why governments fail to act to political science and public administration. My argument is that, no matter what the reasons, governments are still to blame. This book is designed to encourage us to stop blaming people and start blaming governments.

It can still be argued, however, that I make policy prescriptions. I blame the government for bad outcomes as though the cause of the ill is obvious and the solution almost equally so. To make my argument clear, I have tried to choose cases where the causes of the problems are indeed obvious and where we can readily see solutions – although as we go through the five policy chapters, the issues become more complex and the solutions less clear. However, does the public choice critique not also have a normative conclusion? That because government is self-interested and in the pay of lobbies it should be restricted?

The empirical critique can be used equally against the normative solution of standard public choice minimal government and against a larger role for regulatory government. If it is in the interests of government to act as it does, then we cannot expect it to do otherwise. When government regulates, it is because the government has been captured by the industry and works in their interests; when it deregulates, it must be because that is what the industry wants. Indeed, de-regulation and, for example, self-regulation, seems clearly more in the interests of corporations than stricter regulation. In whose interest was the de-regulation of the finance industry that led to the global financial crisis? It was financiers who made the money, and it was financiers who did not suffer the consequences. The constant pursuit of lower taxes in the name of smaller government is directly in the interests of the multimillionaires that dominate US politics in Congress and in the presidency. It is in the interests of the increasingly rich ministers in parliamentary democracies and clearly in the interests of those who support them financially and through the main media, both traditional and social, that exist today.

I do not assume that government is benevolent; quite the contrary. I am calling it out. It is you, the government: the ills of society are your fault. Fess up and take responsibility. My argument is perfectly in keeping with the public choice tradition. We might also note that, in fact, the public choice argument that when government does regulate it does so in the interests of the industry is not supported by empirical literature. Most of the public choice writers have cherry-picked examples to support their case, but more systematic analysis does not support their simplistic theoretical modelling.

Freedom and autonomy

There are two arguments that can be made about the nanny state. The first is that if the state regulates it reduces individual freedom. The second is that it does not respect individual autonomy.

Freedom

There is an obvious sense in which regulation – that is, passing laws that restrict the actions of agents in society – restricts freedom. However, we cannot simply assume that therefore each piece of regulation restricts individual freedom in total. The justification for having a government is that overall it gives people more freedom, safety and welfare.

Regulations can open up freedoms. Regulating gun sales restricts individual freedom to buy guns. Ensuring that guns are not sold to those with psychological problems, perpetrators of domestic violence and other criminals will mean that such people will not be able to legally purchase guns, thereby restricting their freedom. Stopping private sales restricts gun owners in selling their weapons, making people wait a week from ordering to receiving their weapon restricts their ability to use them immediately and banning some types of automatic or semi-automatic weapons prevents anyone from buying such weapons. However, such regulations also increase other freedoms. Being killed or severely injured or threatened by someone with a gun reduces the freedom of the victim. We need to look carefully at the precise effects of regulation before we can judge whether a given regulation reduces or increases the amount of freedom in society. Plus, of course, restricting freedom on the grounds of other values such as safety or welfare might be justified. We cannot assume regulations restrict liberty overall; they often increase liberty overall. If you think liberty is the most important value, one must look at each regulation individually in context to see its effects on that which you value most in society.

What about regulating food manufacture? Regulating food manufacture most directly affects the corporations that produce the products and the companies that sell them. These are not individuals, so it does not directly affect individual liberty. Of course, it will also change the products that consumers can buy. Do such changes restrict liberty? Well, this does not have the easy answer that many seem to think. If freedom is measured by the number of alternatives available, then it might have no effect. Some products are no longer available, new ones are. Indeed, given one can add sugar and salt to products purchased, but one cannot remove them, it gives more opportunities for consumers to have a greater number of products. However, liberty is surely not only about the number of alternatives, but their quality. If the quality is enhanced then again this ought to increase liberty

But don't regulations increase price? Not necessarily: restricting the sugar in carbonated drinks will not increase their price. But if regulations do tend to increase price, then people might buy less. That might decrease their liberty (though it might increase their welfare). If they spend more on food, they will have less to spend on other things, again decreasing liberty. On the other hand, obese people are often restricted in what they are physically able to do. Massively reducing the number of obese people in society might increase the number of activities that people overall can do. Again, the point is we simply cannot tell. We need to look at specific regulations and calculate their likely consequences. The abstract arguments of philosophers are really irrelevant to these empirical questions.

This is one lesson for political philosophy that this book is designed to address. Political philosophers too often rely upon casual analogies. If they were to actually examine social policies in more detail and then to consider what their deep-rooted moral arguments mean for these policies, then we could develop more of a sense of what liberty means in society. In what sense is it paternalistic for governments to provide social housing, when it is not paternalistic for them not to provide social housing? Am I more or less paternalistic when I say to my child who is being bullied at school, 'you need to stand up for yourself' than if I say, 'we shall speak to the headteacher about this'? Is it not just as paternalistic for government to provide tax breaks for home owners as to subsidize rents by building social homes without making a profit? Why is it paternalistic to limit the amount or to tax excess sugar and salt in food products?

The assault upon the welfare state over the past 40 years is made easier if we can blame individuals for all their own ills. If the source of homelessness is lack of forethought or laziness or bad decisions, then the state need not concern itself with providing affordable housing for all. If poorer people are unhealthy and do not live so long because they eat unhealthy food and live unhealthy lives, this just shows that they lack the moral worth of living better. At the same time as the veneration of personal responsibility is peddled by politicians, aided by the philosophical establishment, large-scale corporations manipulate individual choices and work to suppress information that is vital for responsible choice. Food manufacturers fight to keep clear information about their products off their packaging. They fight to be able to advertise unhealthy food to children. And governments let them do so.

Autonomy

One of the big debates in political philosophy with regard to the paternalistic state is respecting people's autonomy. Autonomy in this literature means something like having the capacity to think and decide for yourself. It is sometimes said that autonomous people are authors of their own lives. Regulation might be thought to affect autonomy to the extent that it makes it more difficult for people to be in control of their lives precisely because it regulates them. We might note, however, that what regulation does is to change the incentives for people to behave in one manner or another. It does not affect, at least in the types of regulations I have been discussing, people's abilities to think for themselves or author their lives given the incentives around them. Regulations of the sort I have been discussing do not affect autonomy differently to how they affect freedom.

Autonomy in the paternalist literature has received a lot of attention recently because of the nudge agenda. I discuss this in the next section; nudge is the idea that government does not regulate or tax in order to help people, but rather to give information and to frame decisions in ways that make it more likely that people will make choices which are better for their welfare. Some argue that this does not respect people's autonomy. Nudge assumes that people must be failing in some way to make good decisions about their well-being. They might. But that is not the major concern I have been addressing. It is not that people are failing to make good decisions, it is rather they do not have the opportunity to do so. One cannot buy fresh fruit and vegetables if they are not available, or live in a habitable dwelling if it is not affordable. People who live in food deserts provide one of the starkest examples of the lack of the opportunity to make good decisions. Children who get shot dead are another. State action and state regulation is not about intervening because people are failing to make decisions about their well-being or their wider interest, or failing to have ends they ought to have; it is because they are not being given the opportunity to make such decisions. The state needs to regulate in the manner I am suggesting because too many people do not have the liberties that will enable them to make these decisions.

These are reasons why I think this book is one of political philosophy (as well as public policy). There is a serious disconnect between the sorts of arguments that political philosophers come up with and the political issues of the day that concern public policy. Virtually all discussion of paternalism in political philosophy misses the point about regulation. It is not about not trusting people to act responsibly, since they can only act responsibly in terms of the choices they have. Regulation is about giving them better choices. If they have better choices, then they have the chance to act more responsibly.

Nudge

One response to the informational problems that consumers face in real markets is to suggest that governments need to provide information. This has led to the nudge movement. Behavioural economists and social psychologists have found experimentally that one can change people's behaviour not only by giving information, but by how information is provided (framing). They argue, accordingly, that government can nudge people into better behaviours. So we find signs by the road suggesting drivers slow down. We make pension schemes opt out rather than opt in.

Governments love this notion. They can spend relatively small amounts of money on such nudges, and then continue to blame people for their poor lifestyles. It is the perfect blame-shifting strategy for governments. Nudge follows the ideology that people must take responsibility for their own actions. Thaler and Sunstein, who invented nudge in its modern form, call it 'libertarian paternalism' on the grounds that it does not force people to behave well. But of course, taxation does not force people to behave differently either; it just changes their incentives. When workers have to opt out rather than opt in to a company pension scheme, they are much more likely to stay in the pension scheme – which is in their long-term interest. Thaler and Sunstein make the point that, nevertheless, governments are as likely to create opt-in schemes as opt-out ones.

I am not opposed to nudge as such. To be sure, how we frame alternatives is important. However, it is applicable only to a limited set of situations, and there is a danger that nudging is only a short-term solution. Studies of workplace incentive schemes, such as bonuses, have shown that they only work in the short term. Over time their effects diminish. For some types of incentives, the benefits seen early in the process actually lead to worse long-term outcomes than the control group – it is as though people compensate for their earlier good behaviour by behaving worse later on.

The type of nudge might be important, too. Drivers will stop paying attention to regularly seen roadside speed warnings. However, making pension schemes opt out rather than opt in might achieve the desired long-term results. And for good reason. Both opting in and opting out of pension schemes incur costs. The costs might not be high, but they are costs, so placing them where they act as an obstacle to the undesired behaviour ensures the right incentives.

I do not think the nudge agenda will make the kind of material difference that its proponents hope for. Nudge is fine for the little things in life, such as designing the right wording for letters from tax agencies, but it has been shown to have only marginal effects on big issues like health. Even in areas like anti-smoking campaigns, nudging, while effective, has worked alongside high taxation and banning smoking in the workplace and public buildings and spaces. These regulatory and tax policies have been more effective than merely information on health dangers – indeed, some survey studies suggest that smokers overestimate the health risks of smoking. And I've yet to meet a nudger who thinks that the suicide, accident, murder and mass murder rates in the US would improve if only they had more effective gun nudge campaigns. The big issues need regulation.

Moreover, I take the view that if we agree that one sort of behaviour is better for people, why nudge them into that behaviour rather than regulate them? Why nudge people into pooling their future risk into private or company pensions schemes rather than pooling the risk of everyone into a compulsory state scheme? The usual answer is that we want people to take responsibility for their own future risks. However, the very reason we are framing decisions in such a way that people are more likely to do 'the right thing' is because we have accepted that they are not fully responsible for their choices. I think we will also find that those who campaign the hardest against the pooling of social risk in society as a whole are those who do not need to pool their risk; they already have their own schemes for themselves. The problem of the nudge agenda is that it is a sticking plaster for a minor cut when the body needs major surgery on several vital organs. I am interested by how much time and energy academics have given to the nudge agenda, rather than considering the major social problems our societies face.

A similar argument is often used against government regulation in some industries, and especially professions – better to let the industry self-regulate than to force regulation upon it. However, to the extent that an industry is prepared to self-regulate, why not make those rules state regulations with the stronger force of law behind them? And, as is often the case, when we think that the industry regulations are not sufficient protection, why not regulate further?

Governments do not fail as badly as I portray

A rather different criticism is that governments do rather better overall than I give them credit for. To be sure, not all government initiatives are failures, and I used some examples to illustrate how we might do better. There are plenty of success stories for governments too. We must be aware that even when governments have policies that work well, there will still be issues and problems to address. There will always be a certain number of people who sleep rough, at least occasionally, and most people will never attain what they might think is their 'ideal home'. There will always be some sort of recreational drugs problem and problem gamblers, no matter what governments do, and some people are going to suffer weight and other health problems. Governments ought sometimes to be proud of their achievements – and we can note our governors usually do claim credit when things go well. There might be a 'natural rate' of certain things that governments can never improve upon, but we might never be able to judge what that rate is. That is why we need comparative analysis. Were things better in the past, and can we go back to those better times? Is the situation better in another country, and can we learn from it? I am simply criticizing governments for blaming their citizens for their problems when those are government created. And that really is the bottom line. Governments must take responsibility for their policies at whatever level of success they achieve.

Social responsibility

I have placed the burden of responsibility on governments, but in democracies governments ought to reflect the views of their citizens. The failures I examine are societal failures, not governmental ones. Responsibility ultimately rests with people and not their governments.

We might first ask, why don't people blame the government as I have been doing? Well, of course, many of them do. It is the commentators, the political elites, that often prefer to blame people. But there is a good reason why the personal responsibility mantra works well. Why don't people see the fairly obvious points I've been making about the distribution and structure of problems? Why do they allow blame to be laid on individuals? It is because it is easy for us to see others making mistakes despite our advice, or to realize that we have made some bad choices. So these individual failures are obvious and might, sometimes, be accompanied by a suppressed moral outrage. What we do not see for most people around us is their past histories, and the reasonable choices they made, given their circumstances, that led them to where they are now. We do not see the structures that makes some outcomes so common.

All the way through this book I have been saying that the results of government's regulatory policy is the government's responsibility. I have helped myself to the idea of 'the government'. It might be objected that, in a democracy, people vote and they get the government they have chosen, according to their votes and the rules by which those votes are counted. So, really, the outcomes of governmental regulation are the responsibility of society.

I have no particular desire to argue against that view. We can equally blame ourselves for the regulatory policies of the government. However, rhetorically, I do not think it useful to place responsibility with 'the people'. Many of us can wriggle out of our responsibility on the grounds that we did not vote for the party or coalition that governs. Or that, even though we did vote for this government, we do not agree with *this* policy, but we are forced to vote for the bundle of policies that each party signs up to in their manifestoes and election addresses. And anyway, we only voted for the party that was not as bad as all the others, and not for a government we really wanted. And so on.

The government, understood as those men and women elected to positions on the manifesto they signed up for, and for the policies they enact or refuse to enact, has to take final responsibility. It is no excuse, after all, for a politician to say that while she agrees that it would be better for all recreational drugs to be legalized (and virtually all politicians, senior public servants and police officers I know privately say this), it would be electoral suicide to stand on that policy. For then the politician is saying, I am putting my career first, and the policy I admit is superior to the one we defend second. They still need to take responsibility for the policies that their government enacts and the policies their government does not change.

Governments can wriggle a little bit, just as their voters can. The UK has a strong centralized national government, whereas both the US and Australia have federal governments. I have not much alluded to that in this book. But, for example, housing policy in the US and Australia is largely devolved to the states, though the federal government plays a major role. So politicians can look across to other governments and blame them. If this was a book on the details of policy in any of the areas I've looked at, in any of these countries, then I would spend time considering the coordination problems that cause difficulties. Where coordination problems exist, it is sometimes difficult to assign blame to individual parties; it is hard to judge which agent is most to blame. However, it is not impossible. Coordination and collective action problems are problems, not impossibilities; governments simply have to work together more carefully.

Government is also more than the president, the prime minister and cabinet, or the legislature. It is also the thousands of public employees whose job it is to deliver services and to advise government. Implementation is not always straightforward. Indeed, policy formation is also policy implementation: if one does not set up the correct instruments to carry out a policy, no matter how well meaning that policy is, the policy will fail. We can point the finger at our public servants if they fail in their duties – but, again, we have to look to those at the top to put in place the right procedures and the right people (though generally speaking it is the former which are to blame when policy breaks down). There are complexities in assigning responsibility sometimes, but the government – the people at the top – needs to take ultimate responsibility. As one former US president famously displayed on his desk: the buck stops here.

A paradigm for other issues?

I have chosen issues for which the evidence is fairly clear. There are other issues for which evidence is also clear. I have also chosen issues where the types of policy recommendations I make also seem reasonably clear. Other issues are much harder to grapple with, both because it is less clear what we want to achieve, and how we could achieve those ends (whatever they are) successfully. One big issue, which might in the end make all others seem trivial, is climate change. Of course, no single government can act to achieve what we require in order to survive as a species long term on this planet. They need to act in concert, and that means cooperation on a global scale, probably with sanctions against any country that does not cooperate. Achieving this seems, at the current juncture, somewhat hopeless.

Climate change policy is a paradigm in some ways as to why we need government. It is a global collective action problem that will need all governments to work together, and collective action is often hard to achieve, no matter how important the benefits. It is also a paradigm for some of the problems I have been identifying. It is one where clear scientific evidence has been massively ignored by governments and attacked by vested interests, people who make money out of those things which cause climate change and are rich enough to think they can survive whatever the climate throws at us. It is also an area where academics, opinion-leaders and policy makers have spent far too long and much too much effort asking people to do something about it, whether it is to recycle, use less plastic, walk rather than drive or to take fewer flights, when governments through regulatory actions could make all such personal activity seem trivial. We have a situation where we subsidize airline fuel costs in comparison to other forms of transport, while asking people to consider flying less. So governments provide economic incentives to fly more, while nudging people to fly less. There could hardly be a better example of the ludicrous situation to which the ideology of libertarianism has led us.

Final final word

Suppose any politician in the US – president, senators, congressmen, governors, state senators or assemblymen – or indeed any US citizen, after any gun massacre, or faced with the statistics of the number of gun deaths whether by crime, or suicide or accident, were to say, 'Look, we know this is a terrible event, we know these figures are bad, but they are as they are because we believe that our citizens have the right to buy assault weapons and guns of their choosing under the regulations we currently have. I defend those rights, I defend those laws, and I take full responsibility for the consequences. We have to accept that these massacres, these gun deaths are part of the American way of life, because our gun laws are a part of the American way of life.' Were any politician to openly acknowledge that this is the price and they are prepared to pay that price, then I would give them my respect. I will think their judgement awry, I wouldn't vote for them and I would campaign against them if I lived in the US and had that right. But I would respect them. Any politician, or indeed citizen, who defends the current US gun laws without making such an explicit acknowledgement deserves no respect. I will not give my respect to people who will not take responsibility for their actions.

Notes

Chapter 2

[1] The information about gun laws and all figures go up to the end of 2018, the last full year before the final draft of this book. New Zealand introduced new gun legislation in 2019 to tighten up the law following the gun massacre of 51 Muslim worshippers in Christchurch by a white supremacist terrorist. It involves banning semi-automatic weapons and a registry to track all legally purchased firearms.

Chapter 6

[1] People are often confused about the difference between cannabis, marijuana and hemp. Usage varies. Cannabis and marijuana are essentially different names for the same product derived from the plant species *Cannabis sativa* which comes in several different varieties. 'Cannabis' comes from Middle Eastern usage, 'marijuana' from Asia. US law defines hemp as the stalks, stems and sterilized seeds of the cannabis sativa plant. The compounds (essentially tetrahydrocannabinol (THC)) that have physical and psychological effects are produced from the flowers and leaves. 'Marijuana' is often used for high-THC varieties of cannabis sativa. Those low in THC are sometimes called 'hemp', as the THC cannot be extracted in high enough values to produce the psychological effects. I will use the terms marijuana and cannabis interchangeably, using the spelling marihuana occasionally when referring to government Acts that spell it thus.

[2] Although, in my opinion (I will not argue the case here), there needs to be much stricter quality control testing in the medical drug market. Government should be more directly involved in testing drugs, with much higher legal costs for researchers and firms that hide inconsistent results.

Sources

Chapter 1: Responsibility

Page 1: For the Joe Hockey and Malcolm Turnbull quotes see Joe Hockey: https://www.smh.com.au/politics/federal/joe-hockeys-advice-to-first-homebuyers--get-a-good-job-that-pays-good-money-20150609-ghjqyw.html; Malcolm Turnbull: https://www.theguardian.com/australia-news/2016/may/04/malcolm-turnbull-defends-his-personal-tax-record-and-negative-gearing-policy.

For figures on gun deaths in the US see GunPolicy.org; https://www.gunpolicy.org/firearms/. See Chapter 2 where gun crime is discussed in more detail.

Obesity figures are from the World Health Organisation: http://www.who.int/health-topics/obesity#tab=tab_1 and https://ourworldindata.org/causes-of-death, as well as individual government reports; also see Y. Claire Wang et al, 'Health and economic burden of the projected obesity trends in the USA and the UK', *The Lancet*, 378 (2011), pp 815–25.

Pages 2–3: The idea of the welfare state being popular because the war affected everyone is suggested in Robert E. Goodin and Julian Le Grand, *Not only the poor: the middle classes and the welfare state*, Routledge, 1987.

Peter John, *Analyzing public policy*, Routledge, 2012, describes how our views of policy success change over time.

Page 3: Blame shifting by governments has been extensively studied: for example, Christopher Hood, *The blame game*, Princeton University Press, 2013.

Page 4: There are myriad examples of the dangers of the nanny state, from the academic to the popular. One of the most sensible books on the issue, which gives a clear description and analysis of paternalism, is Julian Le Grand and Bill New, *Government paternalism: nanny state or helpful friend?* Princeton University Press, 2015.

A furious account of government – notably the British Labour government – abrogating responsibility through the cult of personal responsibility appears in Brian Barry, *Why social justice matters*, Polity, 1995.

Page 5: The Robert Kane quote on page 5 comes from his *A contemporary introduction to free will*, Oxford University Press, 2005, p 6. This book is probably the best introduction to modern accounts of free will, and thus to aspects of responsibility. It is a good place to start for the issues of free will and determinism I shy away from in this book.

Pages 8–12: *Personal responsibility*
Over the past 40 years moral and political philosophers have increasingly turned their attention to the freedom and responsibility of citizens. Moral philosophers have debated the nature of free will, while libertarianism and critiques of the paternalist state have taken centre stage. And it is not just right-wing philosophers who have become enamoured of personal responsibility. For the Left, what matters is how far individual outcomes are beyond personal responsibility and how much they are within individual control. The discussion is often couched in terms of luck. The distinction between the sorts of luck we ought to take account of was introduced by Ronald Dworkin; see, for example, his *Sovereign virtue: the theory and practice of equality*, Cambridge University Press, 2000. It is well discussed in John Roemer, *Theories of distributive justice*, Harvard University Press, 1996, though this book is not an easy read. For an extended

argument about the intertwining of luck, talent, responsibility and perceptions of people, see the chapters 'Luck, equality and responsibility' and 'Luck and leadership' in Keith Dowding, *Power, luck and freedom*, Manchester University Press, 2017.

On determinism that still allows the assignation of responsibility to people, see, for example, Daniel Dennett, *Freedom evolves*, Allen Lane, 2003, or Christian List, *Why free will is real*, Harvard University Press, 2019.

Andy Clark, *Mindware: an introduction to cognitive science*, Oxford University Press, 2001, is still a good introduction to autonomy as seen in artificial intelligence and robotics.

Like Dennis on pages 8–12, rough sleepers often blame themselves, making comments similar to those I've invented in this chapter. For more on this issue see Chapter 4.

Page 13: The quote on page 13 about markets leading to the common good comes from a standard handbook: Allen M. Feldman, 'Welfare economics' in John Eatwell (ed.), *The world of economics*, W. W. Norton, 1991.

Page 15: The idea that all failure is government failure can be seen in William R. Keech and Michael C. Munger, 'The anatomy of government failure', *Public Choice*, 164 (2015), pp 1–42.

Information about failed states can be found in N. Ezrow and E. Frantz, *Failed states and institutional decay: understanding instability and poverty in the developing world*, Bloomsbury Academic Press, 2013. For the importance of good institutions of governance, see Daron Acemoglu and James A. Robinson, *Why nations fail: the origins of power, prosperity and poverty*, Profile Books, 2012.

Page 16: *Normative political philosophy*
For my philosophical readers, when I say 'political philosophy needs to be about what governments and societies can do, not what we would like to achieve', I am saying its subject ought to

be non-ideal theory or even what Gerry Cohen called 'rules of regulation', without denying that we can have fact-free moral principles to guide us: G. A. Cohen, *Rescuing justice and equality*, Harvard University Press, 2008, pp 307ff.

Page 19: *Meta-analysis and systematic review*
Michael Borenstein et al, *Introduction to meta-analysis*, John Wiley and Sons, 2009, and Mark Pettigrew and Helen Roberts, *Systematic reviews in the social sciences: a practical guide*, Blackwell, 2006, provide good introductions.

Chapter 2: Gun Crime
Page 26: Table 2.1 was compiled by the author using data from Pew Center (2017) http://www.pewresearch.org/fact-tank/2017/06/22/key-takeaways-on-americans-views-of-guns-and-gun-ownership/, Mother Jones (2019) https://www.motherjones.com/politics/2012/07/mass-shootings-map/ and the Gun Violence Archive (2020) https://www.gunviolencearchive.org/methodology.

Pages 27–8: *US*
Trump's proposal to arm teachers was widely reported: see for example https://www.telegraph.co.uk/news/2018/02/21/donald-trump-proposes-arming-teachers-stop-future-school-shootings/.

For the NRA reactions to massacres and changing gun laws (page 27), and Marco Rubio's and Matt Bevin's claims (page 28) see https://www.nbcnews.com/storyline/orlando-nightclub-massacre/how-nra-has-responded-mass-shootings-over-years-n592551, and also https://www.apnews.com/d9e2f6f20c6c48869109c5f4a5d6d348. This also contains data on gun ownership. US citizens' attitudes to guns (page 28) from the Pew Center, http://www.pewresearch.org/fact-tank/2017/06/22/key-takeaways-on-americans-views-of-guns-and-gun-ownership/; the BBC, https://www.bbc.com/news/world-us-canada-41488081; and Mother Jones, https://www.motherjones.com/politics/2012/07/mass-shootings-map/.

Page 30: For general figures on gun violence, consult https://www.gunviolencearchive.org/methodology. Table 2.1 was compiled from these archives. For evidence comparing the US with other countries, P. Cook and J. Ludwig, *Gun violence: the real costs*, Oxford University Press, 2006; Vladeta Ajdacic-Gross et al, 'Changing times: a longitudinal analysis of international firearm suicide data', *American Journal of Public Health*, 96 (2006), pp 1752–5.

Page 32: For evidence on differential impacts of gun laws in the US (page 32), see Gary Kleck et al, 'Does gun control reduce violent crime?', *Criminal Justice Review*, 41 (2016), pp 488–513; see also R. A. Hahn et al, 'Firearms laws and the reduction of violence: a systematic review', *American Journal of Preventive Medicine*, 28 (2005), pp 40–70; and John R. Lott, Jr, *More guns, less crime: understanding crime and gun-control laws*, 3rd edn, University of Chicago Press, 2010.

Page 33: The quote on differential effects of gun regulations on suicide in the US comes from Antonio Andrés and Katherine Hempstead, 'Gun control and suicide: the impact of state firearm regulations in the United States, 1995–2004', *Health Policy*, 101 (2011), pp 95–103, on p 100.

Page 34: For evidence on the insurance market in the US, see Jean Lemaire, 'The cost of firearm deaths in the United States: reduced life expectancies and increased insurance costs', *Journal of Risk and Insurance*, 72 (2005), pp 359–74.

Pages 34–9: For comparative evidence on gun regulations, see GunPolicy.org, https://www.gunpolicy.org/firearms/.

Page 35: Table 2.2 was compiled by the author from GunPolicy.org (2020) https://www.gunpolicy.org/firearms/ and Vox (2017) https://www.vox.com/2016/2/29/11120184/gun-control-study-international-evidence.

Page 37: Table 2.3 was compiled by the author from GunPolicy.org (2020), Vox (2017) https://www.vox.

com/2016/2/29/11120184/gun-control-study-international-evidence and Julian Santaella-Tenorio et al, 'What do we know about the association between firearm legislation and firearm-related injuries?', *Epidemiologic Reviews*, 38 (2016), pp 140–57.

Pages 39–41: The systematic review discussed is Julian Santaella-Tenorio et al, 'What do we know about the association between firearm legislation and firearm-related injuries?', *Epidemiologic Reviews*, 38 (2016), pp 140–57. I have also used evidence from Zack Beauchamp, 'A huge international study of gun control finds strong evidence that it actually works', https://www.vox.com/2016/2/29/11120184/gun-control-study-international-evidence. For the 2007 Missouri repeal, see D. Webster et al, 'Effects of the repeal of Missouri's handgun purchaser licensing law on homicides', *Journal of Urban Health*, 91 (2014), pp 293–302, 598–601.

Page 41: *Suicide*
For the effects of gun laws on suicide, see M. Miller et al, 'The epidemiology of case fatality rates for suicide in the northeast', *Annals Emergency Medicine*, 43 (2004), pp 723–30; E. Michael Lewiecki and Sara A. Miller, 'Suicide, guns, and public policy', *American Journal of Public Health*, 103 (2013), pp 27–31; and Vladeta Ajdacic-Gross et al, 'Changing times: a longitudinal analysis of international firearm suicide data', *American Journal of Public Health*, 96 (2006), pp 1752–5.

Pages 41–3: *Australian case study*
Simon Chapman et al, 'Association between gun law reforms and intentional firearm deaths in Australia, 1879–2013', *JAMA*, 315 (2016), pp 291–9.

Christine Neill and Andrew Leigh, 'Do gun buy-backs save lives? Evidence from time series variation', *Current Issues in Criminal Justice*, 20 (2008), pp 145–62.

Data on Victoria, J. Ozanne-Smith et al, 'Firearm-related deaths: the impact of regulatory reform', *Injury Prevention*, 10 (2004), pp 280–6.

Matthew M. Large and Olav B. Nielssen, 'Suicide in Australia: meta-analysis of rates of methods of suicide between 1988 and 2007', *MJA*, 192 (2010), pp 432–7.

Chapter 3: Obesity

The systematic review and meta-analyses I have utilized throughout this chapter include L. Te Morenga et al, 'Dietary sugars and body weight: systematic review and meta-analyses of randomised controlled trials and cohort studies', *British Medical Journal*, 346 (2013), e7492; Maria Luger et al, 'Sugar-sweetened beverages and weight gain in children and adults: a systematic review from 2013 to 2015 and a comparison with previous studies', *Obesity Facts*, 10 (2017), pp 674–93; and Eric A. Finkelstein et al, 'Economic causes and consequences of obesity', *American Review of Public Health*, 26 (2005), pp 239–57.

Page 45: Data on mortality and morbidity can be found at https://ourworldindata.org/causes-of-death.

Page 49: The phrase 'street-level bureaucrat' originally comes from Michael Lipsky; see, for example, his *Street-level bureaucracy*, Russell Sage Foundation, 1980.

Pages 50–2: *Regulations affecting liberty*
If the government regulates the amount of salt or sugar in food, it changes the alternatives in a person's menu of opportunities. This chapter argues that this does not necessarily reduce freedom; it might increase it. In fact, the issue is highly complex. Measuring freedom is not trivial, as it involves considering the number of alternatives, how good the alternatives are and how different or diverse they are. See Keith Dowding and Martin van Hees, 'Freedom of choice' in Paul Anand et al (eds), *The Oxford handbook of rational and social choice*, Oxford University Press, 2009, for a non-technical review of this complex issue.

Pages 52–4: *Crisis of obesity*
Figures from Australia, the UK and the US are from the World Health Organisation, as well as government reports from

each country; Eric A. Finkelstein et al, 'Economic causes and consequences of obesity', *American Review of Public Health*, 26 (2005), pp 239–57; and Y. Claire Wang et al, 'Health and economic burden of the projected obesity trends in the USA and the UK', *The Lancet*, 378 (2011), pp 815–25.

Page 54: For evidence on obesity in children, see Patricia M. Anderson and Kristin F. Butcher, 'Childhood obesity: trends and potential causes', *The Future of Children*, 16 (2006), pp 19–45.

Pages 54–7: *Causes of obesity*
On the role of sugar in weight gain and health, see Maria Luger et al, 'Sugar-sweetened beverages and weight gain in children and adults: a systematic review from 2013 to 2015 and a comparison with previous studies', *Obesity Facts*, 10 (2017), pp 674–93; and Laura A. Schmidt, 'New unsweetened truths about sugar', *JAMA Internal Medicine*, 174 (2014), pp 525–6; G. Watts, 'Sugar and the heart: old ideas revisited', *British Medical Journal*, 346 (2013), e7800; and S. Caprio, 'Calories from soft drinks: do they matter?', *New England Journal of Medicine*, 367 (2012), pp 1462–3.

Page 55: For sugar's direct effect on ill-health, see R. H. Lustig et al, 'The toxic truth about sugar', *Nature*, 482 (2012), pp 27–9; Q. Yang et al, 'Added sugar intake and cardiovascular diseases mortality among US adults', *JAMA Internal Medicine* (2014), doi:10.1001/ jamainternmed.2013.13563.

For evidence of sugar addiction in rats, see C. Colantuoni et al, 'Evidence that intermittent, excessive sugar intake causes endogenous opioid dependence', *Obesity Research* (2002), pp 478–88; and V. Mangabeira et al, 'Sugar withdrawal and differential reinforcement of low rate (DRL) performance in rats', *Physiological Behavior*, 139 (2015), pp 468–73.

Page 57: On food labelling, J. L. Pomeranz, 'The bittersweet truth about sugar labeling regulations: they are achievable and overdue', *American Journal of Public Health* (2012), doi:10.2105/ AJPH.2012.300732.

On food deserts, see for example, https://www.theguardian.com/cities/video/2019/nov/20/theres-food-its-just-not-real-food-inside-americas-hunger-capital-video.

Page 58: On taxing SSBs, see K. D. Brownell et al, 'The public health and economic benefits of taxing sugar-sweetened beverages', *New England Journal of Medicine*, 36 (2009), pp 599–605.

Pages 60–2: John Boswell, *The real war on obesity: contesting knowledge and meaning in a public health crisis*, Palgrave Macmillan, 2016, is one of the more sensible examples of the 'rival narrative' approach.

Pages 59–64: *Judging the evidence*
Examples of the lazy intellectual argumentation with regard to obesity include M. Gard and J. Wright, *The obesity epidemic: science, morality and ideology*, Routledge, 2005; R. A. Epstein, 'What (not) to do about obesity: a moderate Aristotelian answer', *Georgetown Law Journal*, 93 (2005), pp 1361–86; and Linda Courtenay Botteril and Andrew Hindmoor, 'Turtles all the way down: bounded rationality in an evidence-based age', *Policy Studies*, 33 (2012), pp 367–79.

Chapter 4: Homelessness

Page 69: *Politicians blaming citizens for not being able to afford to buy homes*
Joe Hockey quote: https://www.smh.com.au/politics/federal/joe-hockeys-advice-to-first-homebuyers--get-a-good-job-that-pays-good-money-20150609-ghjqyw.html; Tim Gurner: https://www.theguardian.com/lifeandstyle/2017/may/15/australian-millionaire-millennials-avocado-toast-house; Malcolm Turnbull: https://www.theguardian.com/australia-news/2016/may/04/malcolm-turnbull-defends-his-personal-tax-record-and-negative-gearing-policy.

Pages 70–4: Gerald Daly, *Homeless: policies, strategies and lives on the street,* Routledge, 1996, charts the increase in homelessness in the US as an issue that increased dramatically during the 1980s.

Australian Bureau of Statistics, *Census of population and housing: estimating homelessness, 2016,* http://www.abs. gov.au/ausstats/abs@.nsf/Latestproducts/2049.0Main%20 Features12016?opendocument&tabname=Summary&prodno= 2049.0&issue=2016&num=&view=. The definition quoted from the ABS appears on the first page of the tab 'Explanatory Notes', 'Appendix 1: Definition of Homelessness'.

On affordable home ownership and housing policy more generally, Josh Ryan-Collins, *Why can't you afford a home?* Polity, 2019, is a lovely little book.

Page 71: *On the freedom of rough sleepers*
See, for example, Jeremy Waldron, 'Homelessness and the issue of freedom', *UCLA Law Review,* 39 (1991), pp 295–324.

Pages 72–4: *What is homelessness?*
On the definition of homelessness and comparative research, see V. Busch-Geertsemia et al, *Extent and profile of homelessness in European member states: a statistical update,* FEANTSA, 2016; and Chris Chamberlain and David Mackenzie, 'Understanding contemporary homelessness: issues of definition and meaning', *Australian Journal of Social Issues,* 27 (1992), pp 274–97.

Pages 76–8: *On the US*
US Department of Housing and Urban Development (2017), https://portal.hud.gov/hudportal/HUD?src=/budget; Mitchell Katz, 'Homelessness: challenges and progress', *Journal of the American Medical Association,* 318 (2017), pp 2293–4; W. J. Wyly and D. J. Hammel, 'Islands of decay in seas of renewal: housing policy and the resurgence of gentrification', *Housing Policy Debate,* 10 (1999), pp 711–71; Edward Goetz, 'The transformation of public housing policy, 1985–2011', *Journal of the American Planning Association,* 78 (2012), pp 452–63.

On dismantling public housing for developer profit, see Edward Goetz, '"Where have all the towers gone?" The dismantling of public housing in U.S. cities', *Journal of Urban Affairs*, 33 (2011), pp 267–87.

Pages 77–8: *Race and housing and the New Deal*
The racial aspects of housing policy in the US is not part of my analysis, but to follow that up the reader should consult Richard Rothstein, *The color of law: a forgotten history of how our government segregated America*, W. W. Norton, 2017.

Page 78: On housing policy generally and the bias towards home ownership, see John Landis and Kirk McClure, 'Rethinking federal housing policy', *Journal of the American Planning Association*, 76 (2010), pp 319–48.

On why home ownership is individually rational but socially irrational, Jim Kemeny, *The myth of home-ownership: private versus public choices in housing tenure*, Routledge, 1981.

Pages 78–81: *On the UK*
Miguel Coelho et al, 'The political economy of housing in England', *New Political Economy*, 22 (2017), pp 31–60; Jill Stewart, 'A review of UK housing policy: ideology and public health', *Public Health*, 119 (2005), pp 525–34; Kate Barker, *Review of housing supply: final report – recommendations*, Controller of Her Majesty's Stationary Office, 2004; Isobel Anderson and Regina Serpa, 'The right to settled accommodation for homeless people in Scotland: a triumph of rational policy-making?', *European Journal of Homelessness*, 7 (2013), pp 13–39.

Pages 81–5: *On Australia*
A general book and source of historical information is Patrick Troy, *Accommodating Australians: Commonwealth government involvement in housing*, Federation Press, 2012. Other works used include Andrew Parkin, 'Housing policy' in B. Galligan et al (eds), *Intergovernmental relations and public policy*, Allen and Unwin, 1991; Saul Eslake, 'Australian housing policy: 50 years of failure: submission to the Senate Economics References Committee',

2013, *Affordable Housing Submission 2*; Chris Martin et al, *Housing policy and the housing system in Australia: an overview – report for the Shaping Housing Futures Project*, Housing Futures, University of New South Wales, 2016.

Australia–UK comparison
Gavin Wood et al, 'Life on the edge: a perspective on precarious home ownership in Australia and the UK', *International Journal of Housing Policy*, 17 (2017), pp 201–26.

Pages 86–7: *The US subprime problems and the global financial crisis*
P. Langley, 'Subprime mortgage lending: a cultural economy', *Economy and Society*, 37 (2008), pp 469–94; IMF, *Debt bias and other distortions: crisis-related issues in tax policy*, Fiscal Affairs Department, 2009; V. Ceriani et al, 'The tax system and the financial crisis', *PSL Quarterly Review*, 64 (2011), pp 39–94.

Pages 86–7: *Tax bias in home ownership*
Bad effects recognized in H. Aaron, 'Income taxes and housing', *American Economic Review*, 60 (1970), pp 789–806; and see H. S. Rosen, 'Owner occupied housing and the federal income tax: estimates and simulations', *Journal of Urban Economics*, 6 (1979), pp 247–66; James Poterba, 'Taxation and housing: old questions, new answers', *American Economic Review*, 82 (1992), pp 237–42.

Page 86: Correcting housing tax bias is argued for in, for example, Richard A. Musgrave, 'In defence of an income concept', *Harvard Law Review*, 81 (1967), pp 44–62; W. Vickery, 'Today's task for economists', *American Economic Review*, 83 (1993), pp 1–10.

Page 87: Dan Andrews et al, 'Housing markets and structural policies in OECD countries', *OECD Economic Department Working Papers* 836, Paris, 2011; Giovanni Favara and Jean Imbs, 'Credit supply and the price of housing', *American Economic Review*, 105 (2015), pp 958–92.

On abolishing tax bias towards home ownership with no deleterious effects, see James Mirlees et al, *Tax by design: the Mirlees review*, Oxford University Press, 2011; European Commission, *Possible reforms of real estate taxation: criteria for successful policies*, European Economy Occasional Papers 2012; European Commission, 'Tax reform in EU members states 2013: tax policy challenges for economic growth and sustainability', *European Economy*, 5 (2013).

Pages 88–9: *On Finland*
Nicholas Pleace, 'The action plan for preventing homelessness in Finland 2016–2019: the culmination of an integrated strategy to end homelessness?', *European Journal of Homelessness*, 11 (2007), pp 95–115; Nicholas Pleace, *Housing First report for the European Observatory on Homelessness*, 2012.

Chapter 5: Problem Gambling

A nice book discussing at a general level some of the issues with regard to gambling and regulation is Peter Collins, *Gambling and the public interest*, Praegar, 2003.

Pages 91–2: American Psychiatric Association (APA), *Diagnostic and Statistical Manual of Mental Disorders*, 4th edn (DSM-IV) American Psychiatric Association Press, 2000. (DSM-V was published in 2013, but most gambling researchers refer to DSM-IV, considering it more definitive.)

Page 91: *On the prevalence of gambling*
A recent article suggests that gambling prevalence might be higher than the estimates I give due to selection bias. See Glenn W. Harrison et al, 'The risk of gambling problems in the general population: a reconsideration', *Journal of Gambling Studies*, https. doi.org/10.1007/s10899-019-09897-2, online publication 2018.

Pages 94–101: *Australia*
Australian Institute for Gambling Research, *Australian gambling: comparative history and analysis,* Victorian Casino and Gambling Authority, 1999.

A. C. Jackson et al, 'Using CPGI to determine problem gambling evidence in Australia: measurement issues', *International Journal of Mental Health and Addiction*, 8 (2010), pp 570–82.

Productivity Commission, *Gambling: Productivity Commission Inquiry report*, Australian Government, 2010.

A short review of gambling issues in Australia can be found in Paul Defabbro and Daniel King, 'Gambling in Australia: experiences, problems, research and policy', *Addiction*, 107 (2012), pp 1556–61.

Page 96: *On the welfare gained from gambling*
Matthew Rockloff et al, 'A quantification of the consumer surplus from gambling participation', *Journal of Gambling Studies*, 35 (2019), pp 1147–62.

Pages 100–1: On revenue and other issues in Australia see https://responsiblegambling.vic.gov.au/about-us/news-and-media/latest-edition-australian-gambling-statistics/.

Page 102: *On the neurological basis of gambling addiction*
Don Ross et al, *Midbrain mutiny: the picoeconomics and neuroeconomics of disordered gambling*, MIT Press, 2008.

Page 103: Alex Blaszcynski and Lia Nower, 'A pathway model of problem and pathological gambling', *Addiction*, 97 (2002), pp. 487–99.

Page 104: The study suggesting EGMs lead faster to pathological gambling is found in R. Breen and M. Zimmerman, 'Rapid onset of pathological gambling in machine gamblers', *Journal of Gambling Studies* 18 (2002), pp 31–43. See also Nicki Dowding et al, 'Electronic Gaming machines: are they the "crack cocaine" of gambling?', *Addiction*, 100 (2005), pp 33–45, which is a general review of EGMs.

Pages 105–7: *Evidence from Norway*

Ingeborg Rossow and Marianne Bang Hansen, 'Gambling and gambling policy in Norway: an exceptional case', *Addiction*, 111 (2016), pp 593–8, from which the data and Norwegian evidence is largely taken. See also A. Borch, 'Gambling in the news and the revelation of market power: the case of Norway', *International Gambling Studies*, 12 (2012), 55–67 and H. O. Fekjaer, 'Putting gambling problems on the agenda – some Norwegian experiences', *Journal of Gambling Issues*, 18 (2006), pp 107–109.

Alex Blaszcynski and Lia Nower, 'A pathway model of problem and pathological gambling', *Addiction*, 97 (2002), pp 487–99.

Chapter 6: Recreational Drugs Policy

Page 115: Windlesham in House of Lords as reported by Philip Bean *Legalising drugs: debates and dilemmas*, Policy Press, 2010, p 12; the actual speech can found at https://api.parliament.uk/historic-hansard/lords/1971/jan/14/misuse-of-drugs-bill.

Pages 116–17: *History of drugs in the UK*

Virginia Berridge and Griffith Edwards, *Opium and the people: opiate use in nineteenth-century England*, St Martin's Press, 1981.

Pages 117–20: *History of drugs in the US*

Lisa N. Sacco, 'Drug enforcement in the United States: history, policy, and trends', *Congressional Research Service* 5-7500, 2014; D. Musto, *The American disease: the origins of narcotic control*, Yale University Press, 1999; and Anthony Lowenstein, *Pills, powder, and smoke: inside the bloody war on drugs*, Scribe, 2019.

Pages 120–1: *History of drugs in Australia*

National Drug and Alcohol Research Centre, *The Australian (illicit) drug policy timeline: 1985–2016*, 2016, http://dpmp.unsw.edu.au/resource/drug-policy-timeline 7/11/19.

Page 121: Ken Lay's quote can be found in Nicole Lee and Alison Ritter, 'Australia's recreational drugs policies aren't working, so what are the options for reform?', *The Conversation*, 1 March 2016, https://theconversation.com/australias-recreational-drug-policies-arent-working-so-what-are-the-options-for-reform-55493.

The quote from Mick Palmer can be found in Mick Palmer, 'After 33 years, I can no longer ignore the evidence on drugs', *Sydney Morning Herald*, 7 June 2012, https://www.smh.com.au/politics/federal/after-33-years-i-can-no-longer-ignore-the-evidence-on-drugs-20120606-1zwpr.html.

See also Mick Palmer, Submission to the Queensland Productivity Inquiry into Imprisonment and Recidivism, https://qpc.blob.core.windows.net/wordpress/2019/04/IRDR023-Inquiry-into-Imprisonment-Mick-Palmer.pdf.

Kate Burton, 'Illicit drugs in Australia: use, harm and policy responses', E-Brief: online only issued 17 May 2004, Parliament of Australia, https://www.aph.gov.au/About_Parliament/Parliamentary_Departments/Parliamentary_Library/Publications_Archive/archive/illicitdrugs.

Pages 121–3: *How great a problem?*
A good systematic review of evidence from around the world can be found in Louisa Degenhardt and Wayne Hall, 'Extent of illicit drug use and dependence, and their contribution to the global burden of disease', *Lancet*, 379 (2012), pp 55–70; and Louisa Degenhardt et al, 'The global burden of disease projects: what have we learned about illicit drug use and dependence and their contribution to the global burden of disease?', *Drug and Alcohol Review*, 33 (2014), pp 4–12.

Page 122: 'In Australia ... A 2017 report described': see Australian Bureau of Statistics Media Release, 'Drug induced deaths at highest rate since late 90s', https://www.abs.gov.au/ausstats/abs@.nsf/Lookup/by%20Subject/3303.0~2016~Media%20Release~Drug%20Induced%20Deaths%20Increase%20in%202016%20(Media%20Release)~9.

Pages 123–4: The two quotes from James Q. Wilson, 'Against the legalization of drugs', are in James Incardi and Karen McElrath (eds), *The American drug scene*, 2nd edn, Roxbury, pp 304, 311.

Pages 123–9: *Decriminalization, legalization and regulation*
For general arguments for criminalizing or not criminalizing drug use, see Anthony Culyer, 'Should social policy concern itself with drug use?', *Finance Quarterly*, 1 (1973), pp 449–56; Douglas Husak and Peter de Marnefe, *The legalization of drugs: for and against*, Cambridge University Press, 2006; and Philip Bean, *Legalising drugs: debates and dilemmas*, Policy Press, 2010.

A good review of evidence is found in Michael Grossman et al, 'Illegal drug use and public policy', *Health Affairs*, 21 (2002), pp 134–45.

Page 126: On the economic effects of drug use, Chris Wilkins and Fraik Scrimgeour, 'Economics and the legalization of drugs', *Agenda*, 7 (2000), pp 333–44, which includes the estimates of elasticity on page 126; Anne Line Bretteville-Jensen, 'To legalize or not to legalize? Economic approaches to the decriminalization of drugs', *Substance Use and Misuse*, 41 (2006), pp 555–65; Jeffry A. Miron, 'The economics of drug prohibition and drug legalization', *Social Research*, 68 (2001), pp 835–55.

Pages 127–8: On ending illegal production through the use of excise tax and allocation of resources, see Gary Becker et al, 'The market for illegal goods: the case of drugs', *Journal of Political Economy*, 114 (2006), pp 38–60. For estimates on savings on enforcement, see Jeffrey A. Miron, *Drug war crimes: the consequences of prohibition*, Independent Trust, 2004. The quote from Milton Friedman on page 127 comes from Milton Friedman, 'The war we are losing' in M. B. Krauss and E. P Lazear (eds), *Searching for alternatives: drug control policy in the United States*, Hoover University Press, 1991, pp 53–67.

Pages 129–32: *Portugal*

An excellent and measured article is Caitlin Elizabeth Hughes and Alex Stevens, 'A resounding success or a disastrous failure: re-examining the interpretation of evidence on the Portuguese decriminalization of illicit drugs', *Drug and Alcohol Review*, 31 (2012), pp 101–33. I also used Caitlin Elizabeth Hughes and Alex Stevens, 'What can we learn from the Portuguese decriminalization of illicit drugs?', *British Journal of Criminology*, 50 (2010), pp 999–1022; and Lauren Gallagher, 'Should the United States move towards Portuguese decriminalization of drugs?', *University of Miami International and Comparative Law Review*, 22 (2015), pp 207–32.

Page 133: On the argument that prohibiting drugs has more to do with racism, popular myth, bureaucratic expansion or foreign policy, see, for example, E. Abel, *Marijuana: the first 12,000 years*, Plenum Press, 2000: D. Musto, *The American disease: the origins of narcotic control*, Yale University Press, 1999; and Anthony Lowenstein, *Pills, powder, and smoke: inside the bloody war on drugs*, Scribe, 2019.

Chapter 7: Government Responsibility

Page 138: David Benton, 'Portion size: what we know and what we need to know', *Critical Reviews in Food Science and Nutrition*, 55 (2015), pp 988–1004.

Page 145: *Government not taking account of evidence*

See, for example, Lawrence M. Mead, 'Only connect: why government often ignores research', *Policy Sciences*, 48 (2015), pp 257–72; Joshua Newman et al, 'Policy capacity and evidence-based policy in the public service', *Public Management Review*, 19 (2017), pp 157–74; Paul Cairney, *The politics of evidence-based policy making*, Palgrave Macmillan, 2016.

On the difference between political science and public policy research, see my *The philosophy and methods of political science*, Palgrave, 2016, ch. 10, 'Political science as a vocation'.

Page 146: Jeanine Baker and Samara McPhedran, 'Gun laws and sudden death: did the Australian firearms legislation of 1996 make a difference?', *British Journal of Criminology*, 47 (2007), pp 455–69.

Page 149: Nicki Dowling et al, 'Electronic gaming machines: are they the "crack-cocaine" of gambling?', *Addiction*, 100 (2015), pp 33–45, quote at p 42.

Pages 150–3: *Wicked problems*
Horst W. J. Rittel and Melvin M. Webber, 'Dilemmas in a general theory of planning', *Policy Sciences*, 4 (1973), pp 155–69. A sensible discussion can be found in Brian W. Head and John Alford, 'Wicked problems: implications for public policy and management', *Administration and Society*, 47 (2015), pp 711–39.

There is a vast literature on the trolley problem (the problem isn't 'should you pull the switch?', but rather 'why pull the switch in this case but not in other similar cases?'). Judith Jarvis Thomson, 'The trolley problem', *Yale Law Journal*, 94 (1985), pp 1395–415 is the best place to start and still one of the most sensible discussions.

Joshua Newman and Brian W. Head, 'The national context of wicked problems: comparing policies on gun violence in the US, Canada, Australia', *Journal of Comparative Policy Analysis*, 19 (2017), pp 40–53, discusses gun violence as a wicked 'unsolvable problem' in the US but one readily solvable in other countries.

Pages 154–8: *Government failure*
Most public choice writers still refer back to the classic theoretical arguments. See, for example, Sam Peltzman, 'Toward a more general theory of regulation', *Journal of Law and Economics*, 29 (1976), pp 211–40; Gordon Tullock, 'The costs of special privilege' in James E. Alt and Kenneth A. Shepsle (eds), *Perspectives on positive political economy*, Cambridge University Press, 1990; Gene Grossman and Elhanan Helpman, 'Protection for sale', *American Economic Review*, 84 (1986), pp 89–106.

Empirical evidence showing the problems are not as great as public choice writers claim can be found in Daniel Carpenter and David A. Moss (eds), *Preventing regulatory capture: special interest influence and how to limit it*, Cambridge University Press, 2014.

Pages 158–61: *Freedom and autonomy*
Measuring freedom is not trivial, as it involves considering the number of the alternatives, how good the alternatives are and how different or diverse they are. See Keith Dowding and Martin van Hees, 'Freedom of choice' in Paul Anand et al (eds), *Oxford handbook of rational and social choice*, Oxford University Press, 2009, for a non-technical review of this complex issue.

Pages 160–1: Sarah Conley, *Against autonomy: justifying coercive paternalism*, Cambridge, 2013, suggests autonomy is not all it's cracked up to be.

Page 162: *Nudge*
Cass Sunstein and Richard Thaler set off the nudge fashion in *Nudge: improving decisions about health, wealth and happiness*, Yale University Press, 2008; while Sunstein recognizes the different ways in which nudge can work in 'Nudges that fail', *Behavioral Public Policy*, 1 (2017), pp 4–15. The example of nudging with a letter on tax is from Peter John, *How far to nudge: assessing behavioral public policy*, Edward Elgar, 2018, p 72. Paternalism and nudge are nicely captured in Julian Le Grand and Bill Nice, *Government paternalism: nanny state or helpful friend?*, Princeton University Press, 2015.

There is a large literature on framing. Daniel Kahneman and Amos Tversky (eds), *Choices, values, and frames*, Cambridge University Press, 2000 (especially the opening essay) is a good place to start.

Will Leggett, 'The politics of behaviour change: nudge, neoliberalism and the state', *Policy & Politics*, 42 (2014), pp 3–19, challenges the idea that nudge is libertarian.

Page 164: Joannah Luetjens et al (eds), *Successful public policy: lessons from Australia and New Zealand*, ANU Press, 2019, is a book of government success stories (though I am not sure all will agree with some of the purported successes).

Page 166: *Responsibility in complex settings*
On the difficulties and solutions to assigning responsibility in complex settings, often called the problem of many hands, see Dennis F. Thompson, *Restoring responsibility: ethics in government, business and healthcare*, Cambridge University Press, 2004, or his essay 'Designing responsibility: the problem of many hands in complex organizations' in Jeroen van den Hoven et al (eds), *The design turn in applied ethics*, Oxford University Press, 2017.

Index

Page numbers in *italics* refer to tables.

Body Mass Index (BMI) 48–49,
52
and body-size dispute 50, 52
Buridan's Ass 60
causes of 54–57
and challenges to evidence 59–64
and children 47
crisis of 52–54
discourse analysis 60–61
and dopamine production 46
and experts 63–64
and fats *see* additives
and fat shaming 64, 66–67
and health 52–54
and National Health Service
(NHS) 46
and liberty 51
and responsibility *see* responsibility,
obesity
and rival narratives 60–61, 63
salt *see* additives
sugar 6, 18–19, 46 50–51, 54–56,
57–61, 63, 138, 148, 159, 160
see also additives
sugar-sweetened beverages (SSBs)
54–56
sweeteners *see* additives
and tax 58–59
and UK 53
ultra-processed food 56
and US 52, 56
opportunity 5

P

paternalism 22, 113–114
pharmaceutical industry 156
planning disasters 3
political philosophy 16–18, 156,
157, 159–161
and ideal/non-ideal theory 17
privatization 3
public choice theory 154–155,
157–158

R

regulation 16, 160–164
reducing freedom 150–160
regulatory capture 16, 154–155,
157
rent-seeking 154–155
respect 168

responsibility 1–24, 135–168
and biology 5, 47–48
and comparative choice situations
8–12, 62
deflecting to people 59
and drugs 142–143
and fat shaming 64, 66–67
and forces beyond our control 5
and gambling 92, 96–97, 101–
104, 108, 109, 110, 141–142
and gun laws 44, 136–137
of government 4, 12–16, 52, 57,
59, 64–66, 69–72, 74–76, 87, 90,
109, 110, 113–114, 117, 135–168
avoidance due to unsolvable
problems 150–153
individual members of 166
and homelessness 8–12, 72,
69–72, 74–76, 87, 90, 139–141,
144
and incentives 63
level of 4
and neurology 5
and obesity 46–48, 59, 64–66,
137–139
and opportunity set 6
personal responsibility 4, 8–12,
23, 59, 62–64, 64–66, 69, 92,
96–97, 101–104, 108, 109, 110,
159–160, 165–166, 168, 172–173
peddled by politicians 160
and political philosophy 17,
159–160
and regulation 66–67, 160–161
and risk enjoyment 50, 92
social responsibility 164–166
and statistical relationships 48, 62
and type *see* type
risk 2, 10, 50, 96–97, 163
Rittel, Horst 150

S

Santaella-Tenorio, Julian 39
science and scientific evidence 145,
155
shock jocks 143
social responsibility *see* responsibility,
social responsibility
special interests 154–156
strong state 14–15
Sunstein, Cass 162